For Dear Valentine —
In Friendship.
Shalom!

Herbert Samuel
Jun. '80

MOTTELE

MOTTELE

A PARTISAN ODYSSEY

BY Gertrude Samuels

HARPER & ROW, PUBLISHERS

New York, Hagerstown, San Francisco, London

FIRST EDITION

Designed by Sidney Feinberg

Library of Congress Cataloging in Publication Data

Samuels, Gertrude.
  Mottele.: a partisan odyssey.
  1. Shlayan, Mottele—Fiction.
PZ4.S1926Mo3   [PS3569.A4668]   813'.5'4   75–25101
ISBN 0–06–013759–2

---

76 77 78 79 10 9 8 7 6 5 4 3 2 1

For Benjamin and Julie

AUTHOR'S NOTE

This documentary novel is based on the lives and deeds of Jewish partisans who fought in the forests of Poland and the Soviet Union in World War II. Where it seemed relevant, the real names of certain partisans have been used. I chose to use history-as-novel for a number of reasons.

There is a body of evidence today about the true role and worth of World War II partisans, notably the Jewish partisans —evidence in the Yad Vashem Institute in Israel; the Ghetto Fighters House in Israel; the YIVO Institute for Jewish Research in New York; the Wiener Library in London; and among ex-partisans themselves. In gathering research and interviews to document this book, I decided to focus on one boy's extraordinary contribution to the strange partisan odyssey through the Holocaust, in the general context of the war.

It is now three decades since the Nazis tyrannized Europe with their ambitions for a "thousand-year Reich." In the dozen years that Hitler's Reich did exist, his followers killed millions of people; but the genocidal war against the Jews, during which six million of them perished, remains the most sordid chapter of World War II.

A new generation has grown up since then, with little firsthand knowledge of what really went on.

To some chroniclers of the Nazi evildoers in the ghettos, slave-labor camps, concentration and killing camps, the trouble with the Nazi evil was that it was "banal." Hitler's executioner Eichmann, as revealed in the prisoner's cage in his Jerusalem trial, was "banal." Such an intellectual reaction to the nature of the beast, coming from experts in genocide, has always fascinated me. "Banal" means trivial, commonplace; but can such evil, especially on the Nazi scale, ever be "banal"?

And did all the Jews go "like lambs to the slaughter," that well-publicized cliché? (An expression, incidentally, attributable to the prophet Jeremiah.) Or did those *who could* try to fight for their honor and their lives, as Jews?

Such questions have long concerned many serious students of the Holocaust, both Gentile and Jew. The idea for this documentary novel came, unexpectedly, from a newspaper story about a boy partisan called Mottele (pronounced Mo-'te-le; in Yiddish, מאָטעלע). Mottele seemed to have no last name, no family, no birthplace, and his deeds were surfacing. I felt the pull to know more about Mottele. He was evidently no "lamb."

As a consultant to UNICEF in the 1940's, as a writer on the staff of *The New York Times* who had often "covered" the Displaced Persons camps of Europe and the Holocaust survivors, I could never forget one particular group—the Jewish children of Mottele's age and older (for most Jewish infants were massacred with their mothers) who had managed to survive Auschwitz and Dachau and Bergen-Belsen and Maidanek.

And so I went back recently to certain sites of the Hitler-instituted ghettos and killing centers in Poland, Germany and Austria. My most traumatic experience this time came at the old Maidanek camp near Lublin and the Russian border. It stands just as the Nazis left it, with its acres of barracks, barbed-wire enclosures and watchtowers; a hideous, empty, overgrown, monstrous symbol—of "banality"? I had previously been to the Soviet Union, notably the Ukraine, where Mottele was born, and I have covered the State of Israel many times since its rebirth.

Wherever I went, I sought out Jewish partisans of World War II—those who had fought in the forests and in the ghettos. I am deeply grateful to scores of these men and women of many countries for sharing their experiences, documents and photographs with me; and to the partisan and ghetto-survivors groups, who were cooperative. I want also to express appreciation to the Gildenman family, who showed me the hospitality of their home in Israel; in particular, to Symcha Gildenman, who gave me permission to use extracts, adaptations and direct quotes from his father's writings, and in interviews shared his personal recollections with me.

This history-as-novel approach, using a certain shift in time sequences, afforded the writer the freedom to explore the characters' motivations and ideas in the context of the war. I wanted to go to the roots of reality for the partisans in *their* time; for their reality helps us to understand our present reality. Their odyssey during such "strange, eventful history" is based on true episodes.

G. S.

London
August, 1975

There was a certain Jew in Shushan the castle, whose name was Mordechai the son of Jair . . . a Benjamite . . . [and] Mordechai bowed not down nor prostrated himself before . . . Haman.

ESTHER 2:5, 3:2

1

They had raced their horses back from the sabotage mission, twisting along the forest paths, shielded by ancient oaks and beeches, the dust raised by the horses powdering the tree trunks. They were in great good humor after the success of their mission.

"For every dead German, a live Jew!" Diadia had intoned ritually as he set the last of the explosives that later blew up the bridge—and the German troops driving to the Russian front. He and his son, Lyonka, now carried half a dozen rifles, pistols and a machine gun, taken from the dead hands and breasts of the Germans, and German insignia-of-rank ribbons torn from their uniforms for the swapping later of souvenirs.

Safely back in the forest retreat, racing toward camp, Diadia felt excited, hungry, too, but drained by the act of killing, and thankful that he could endure it.

That was the word—endure.

He sent a look of pride at his son, and Lyonka smiled back. Grimly.

Lyonka had long since disciplined himself not to think about bodies being flung up like aimless arrows. At eighteen, he didn't want to kill men, but he had come to think of the bodies as "missions"—each German a mission to be executed. Experience had taught him not to dwell on it. This mission was finished. It was successful. He and his father lived. He was glad to be alive. He could think again about the living, about Sarah. Exciting, black-haired, long-legged Sarah, with her high color and, he had to remind himself, her talent for driving away any show of tenderness. Sarah the immaculate, he called her privately, dressed like one of the men in her baggy blue shirt and baggy trousers, withdrawn and skeptical still, but warmly alive.

Then Diadia flung open the door of the *budke*, their wooden headquarters, and they saw the boy. Small and fair-haired, he lay asleep by the fire with his legs drawn up nearly to his chin, a sort of fetal bundle. He wore a long, ragged, sacklike coat over his torn shirt and short trousers. He was barefoot, and he held what looked like a wooden violin case very close to him.

The men stared at each other and at the intruder.

"What's this, then?" Lyonka burst out. "A musician for our troops?"

Diadia used the butt of his rifle to stir the boy, who awoke and scrambled to his feet. He held the case tight.

Lyonka was always to remember that even in that first moment of fright, the boy quickly regained his composure and was very polite, but his eyes, of the brightest blue, enormous in the pinched face, were hard and unflinching. He seemed to be trying to make himself look very tall as he stood before the men in his bare feet and his long coat. When he talked, in an even, well-educated voice, he came straight to the point, like an older, resolute person, not like the peasant boy he seemed to be. He spoke in Ukrainian.

"I was told this was a partisan camp," he said. "I want to join the partisans."

The men laughed.

"Where are they?" asked Diadia, his guard up at the mention of partisans.

"I've been looking for them. I want to fight with them."

"Partisans? Where are they, then?"

"Don't *you* know?" the boy replied quietly.

So he can spar like an adult, Lyonka thought with amusement.

"How old are you?" Lyonka asked.

"Old enough. I want to fight with them."

"Come on. How old?"

"Fifteen."

"More like ten," retorted Diadia.

"All right, I'm twelve. But I know a lot, and I can be very useful," the boy said in a hard tone. "I've lived in the forest for months, and I can handle animals, and I ride a horse. I have to be with the partisans."

"Well, why have you come here?"

"I've really been looking for Diadia, the man they call Diadia Misha, Uncle Misha."

Diadia and Lyonka exchanged a look.

"Who's this Uncle Misha?"

"Everyone seems to know about him. I know he's a commander of a—well, a *particular* group in the forest."

"Why just him? There are many partisan groups roaming around these forests."

"I know that. I have to find Uncle Misha," the boy said stubbornly.

"Why?"

"Because."

The boy fell silent, the enormous eyes boring into the two men, but he was clearly worried about proffering his reasons.

"Where are your parents?" asked Diadia.

"Dead."

"And the rest of your family?"

"I have no one."

The boy stared them down, but now he looked from their rifles to the door, as if measuring the distance should he have to run.

"Let's see what's in that case," Diadia said, not unkindly. The boy started to open it, but Lyonka grabbed the case from him and took it outside. Diadia and the boy waited in silence. When, after a moment, Lyonka reentered the *budke*, Diadia's face lit up with pleasure, for Lyonka was holding an old, well-polished violin, its rich cedar wood veined but gleaming. He handed it to the boy, who took it and replaced it, with immense gentleness, in its green felt case, then edged to the door.

"Wait!" Diadia commanded. "What's your name, boy? Where'd you come from?"

"My name is Mitka, and I'm from village Korsnovka in Volhynia. I've been asking everywhere for Uncle Misha."

"When did you leave Korsnovka?"

"Half a year ago, maybe. I'm not sure how long it's been. I've been living in the forest. I got work as a shepherd with some farmers, and they gave me food and places to sleep."

"If you have such work," Diadia persisted, "why look for the partisans and this . . . this Uncle Misha?"

"To fight with his group. To kill Germans!" The boy looked at them defiantly.

"You managed to keep *that* all this time?" Lyonka asked coldly, pointing to the violin.

Since when did peasants own violins? Had this one stolen it, maybe from Jews?

The boy reacted with a show of fierce rebellion now. "I hid it every time I went for work. I found places—in a ditch, or high up in a tree. I have to keep it. It's mine!"

"All right, all right," Diadia interrupted. "You can stay here tonight at least, and eat with us."

The boy seemed suddenly to be very tired, and desperate as a cornered fox. But he no longer looked toward the door.

"Thank you. It's just . . . I've been asking everywhere."

When the men volunteered nothing further, he went back to the fireplace, lay down again and closed his eyes, his arm around the violin case.

The men stood above him, puzzled and suspicious. The boy had made a good impression, but who was he really, this educated, fair-haired, blue-eyed, Ukrainian-speaking fiddler?

Partisans lived by their own law, carefully judging each man and boy. Would this boy tell the Germans about their camp if they let him go? Because of his seeming innocence and youth, had he been chosen deliberately by the enemy to spy and inform on them? Nor was it only Germans that they had to consider: many in the local Ukrainian populace were only too eager to disclose, to the Germans who now occupied the area, partisan hideouts, be they Russian or Polish or Jewish, for a price or for no price. Many times the partisans had to keep intruders with them for weeks, never using their true names or nicknames in the presence of intruders, for fear of betrayal; they let the outsiders go only when they moved camp. It was in this context that Diadia, considering the sleeping boy, felt perplexed but drawn to him.

There were nearly two hundred partisans now under his command. He felt the responsibility every moment of their strange, arduous life in the forest.

Heavy-set, bespectacled, with a middle-aged paunch that hung over his ill-fitting khaki trousers, Diadia had hardly been raised to be a fighting man, a saboteur, a killer; nor was he studied in the psychological arts, to give him instant insight into truth or lies. Until recently he had been, at age forty-four, a civil engineer and businessman in Korets, a small town in the Ukraine, where he was making a substantial living as manager of a cement factory—a civic leader who also loved and wrote music and conducted the orchestra. That was the recent past; but now in the forest, every single consideration boiled down to just one thing—life or death, kill or be killed. He had no room for trigger-shy people, not with some two hundred lives under his protection! And until he was certain of escapees into his camp, he rarely took chances with intruders.

So Diadia Misha's thoughts ran on as he ruminated about this intruder. Most Jewish escapees instinctively concealed their identities: it was well established that certain ethnic bands would as soon kill a Jewish "bandit" as the German enemy. But the exploits of Misha and his partisans, though they were suspected of being all Jewish, had spread over the Polish-Russian border in this area and into the ghettos; Jews knew that whatever their means or age or family size, they would not be hurt or turned away by Diadia Misha's unit. Diadia knew that rumors about his partisans had grown to such proportions that some believed his followers numbered in the thousands. Well, let the Germans believe the rumors, he told his partisans.

The boy puzzled him, with his "Aryan" looks, his reticent "Because," but that night Diadia consulted his deputies and they decided that, at least for the present, the boy should stay on. Partly because they were unsure of him, who spoke such perfect Ukrainian and Russian; partly because he was just a boy, and so many of them had lost their own children.

It was young Sarah who had helped them decide. "What's wrong with having some music in our lives?" she had asked. "Soothe a few of you savages, eh?" And after the laughter had died down, "Anyway, I need another hospital helper. I'm *oysgematert*—exhausted!"

In the days that followed, Mitka was careful to ask nothing further about Diadia Misha, and the men were, in turn, careful about not using their names or nicknames. The boy seemed to understand that they didn't trust him. All the partisans who spoke in his presence used only Ukrainian or Russian. But he waited, and sought some sign.

Meanwhile, he played his violin for them—local folk songs with which he seemed shrewdly to be testing them. Sometimes he sang the songs first, watching their faces, before he played them on the violin: a rousing song of the mountains; a melancholy one recalling memories of when the Ukrainians were free Cossacks—

> "O dear and quiet land,
> O my Ukraine,
> Why do they plunder thee?"

The partisans shifted uneasily with that one. Afterward Sarah sharply ordered him to play Paderewski's "Minuet," one of their favorites.

"I used to play at all kinds of parties and weddings," Mitka answered guardedly when they asked about his curious choice of songs.

For three weeks he went about his assigned chores, volunteering little more about himself. Sarah shortened his coat and she had found him some boots, German boots. It was spring, and the weather was mostly clear, sunny at noon but very cold at night. The boots were miles too big for the boy; he stuffed the toes with rags and kept them on, relishing their warmth so much that some nights he even slept in them.

He felt drawn to Sarah, who was kind to him, and who, when he tried to thank her for the boots, had said, "What about a kiss, little brother?"

Astonished, but deeply moved, he'd reached up to kiss her on the cheek and she'd held him to her briefly, fiercely.

He felt he was under surveillance as he helped to prepare and set the table for the meals, as he calmed and washed down the horses and donkeys after the partisan missions. Sometimes a horse came back without its rider, and then he would stand listening tensely to machine-gun volleys in the forest, feeling an old sickness violently twist his stomach, but he no longer wanted to run. He waited, keeping his feelings buried, executing his chores precisely under the watchful eyes.

And one day when Mitka came into the *budke* he found Diadia holding his violin, plucking at the strings with an expert's ease. Slowly Mitka handed him the bow. Then the little hut was filled not with folk music, but with a soaring Chopin mazurka, followed by some gentle Schubert. Mitka sat by the fireplace in admiration and wonder.

"I could play every instrument in the orchestra," Diadia said abruptly. He ended the concert as suddenly as he had begun it. He put the violin down and left.

The incident almost shook Mitka's resolve to hold back any longer. Such a man as this I can surely trust, the boy argued with himself. Still he hesitated, knowing the dangers of his position if he guessed wrong. Instinctively he felt drawn to the father and his son, but nevertheless kept testing them. Trying to learn more about them.

"I want to be like you," he blurted out one day to Lyonka, surprising him. The boy so far hadn't seemed capable of showing real feelings for anyone.

"Why is that?"

"You're doing things . . . against them!"

"Them?"

"The Nazis. You fight them!"

"We have to find them first," Lyonka said.

"I can be more useful!" The boy's eyes were hard.

"How?"

"I want to be like you! Take my own revenge."

"That's up to the commander," Lyonka said.

"He's your father. Tell him!"

"No one *tells* a commander," Lyonka retorted.

The boy felt the dismissal, and he turned sharply away in case Lyonka should see the tears starting.

Then Mitka finally got the sign he'd been waiting for. He was aware that father and son went off by themselves when they returned from a mission. Mitka regarded such comings and goings with a mixture of curiosity and envy, remembering how once his father had favored *him* with such confidential walks and talks; especially when Mitka returned from his violin lessons in the village next to theirs: then the evenings had glowed for Mitka as he'd basked in his father's awe of his son's learning and his skill on the violin, which the father treasured though he himself couldn't play a note.

One day Mitka determined to follow Lyonka and Diadia. He slipped away from his chores and tailed them until they reached an isolated spot a distance from the camp, where they paused and put on their caps. As Mitka watched from behind a tree, he saw to his astonishment that Diadia had pulled out a small, worn prayer book, which they shared, and he heard them, quite clearly in the forest stillness, start praying in Hebrew. Chanting the Kaddish, the mourner's ancient prayer for the dead:

"Yisgadal v'yiskadash shmei rabo . . ."

At once Mitka stepped out from behind the tree. All the emotions he had kept dammed up for so long burst from him in a flood of recognition and identification and love, and he wept openly as he ran to them, and without fear joined them in the Kaddish. His Hebrew was perfect.

Lyonka had stopped praying, regarding the boy with amazement, as he listened to Mitka's deeply felt chanting; but Diadia went on without pause, taking in the dramatic turn of events with a sudden serene smile. Then he nodded to his son to continue and Lyonka joined in the chanting, his arm around the boy's shoulders.

"My name isn't Mitka," he told them after the prayers. "I'm Mordechai, of the family Shlayan. I'm called Mottele. I didn't want to lie to you, but I was afraid to tell anyone I was Jewish. After my family was killed, I was warned not to use my Jewish name. I kept hearing about Diadia *Misha*, Uncle *Misha*, and that this Uncle Misha was Jewish, and his partisans were Jewish. That was the reason I wanted to find him, to be only with his group. To fight with him!"

"And *we* couldn't quite trust you because you look and act like a typical Gentile—a *shaygetz!*" Lyonka said.

"I had to! I had to play that part! It's the way I've managed to live for months!"

"We couldn't be sure of you. Though you did have me wondering about that violin," Lyonka said, grinning.

"Now you can tell me how to find Diadia Misha?"

"Yes, I can, Mottele," said Lyonka. "You're looking at Diadia Misha. Let me introduce him—my father!"

"Shalom, partisan," said Diadia Misha.

In that momentous year of 1942, Mottele, aged twelve, knew that at last he had found the one world that could have any meaning to him. The dream of the forest, the driving need for vengeance, had become his *only* reality. What had gone before was a nightmare, and in the context of that nightmare Mottele's world had crumbled in ashes.

The Nazis had taken less than three weeks to conquer Poland in September, 1939, and begin the organized persecution of Polish Jews, but it was not until the outbreak of war with Russia, in June, 1941, that Hitler had stepped up his campaign for extermination of the whole Jewish people—in Nazi terms, "the final solution of the Jewish question." In the German-occupied Ukraine, where Mottele had lived, the Nazis coveted the rich grain lands; the herds of cattle; the horses; the immense iron ore and steel industries—resources all for their military machine.

But the Jews were to go first.

In Mottele's village of Korsnovka in the Ukraine, with its small industries and small farms, his father had been a miller.

The peasants would bring their grain to his windmill for grinding. For the most part, Gentile and Jew were courteous to one another, but distant. Mottele's father, a frail, hard-working, religious man who believed intensely in God's will, often worried about that paradox, the mixture of good and bad in the village. ("Every stick has two ends," he would quote from something in a worried way.) But he put his worries aside each week, on the Sabbath, when he celebrated that holy day's joy and peace.

Mottele had gone to *cheder* with the other Jewish boys of the village, he told Diadia Misha, for his Hebrew and academic studies; and once a week he'd gone to the next village for his violin lessons. The old violin was a family heirloom, having belonged to an uncle, long dead, and been handed down to Mottele, who was named for him. Because of Mottele's musical talent, the family Shlayan was occasionally invited to a peasant's wedding or birthday celebration; the whole family had to attend, for this was considered by the peasants a great honor; in fact, they made the Shlayans "honored guests" for the day, and Mottele would play their favorite songs.

"We were often like that, friendly in our village, until war broke out," Mottele said. "Then the police started beating and chasing the Jews. The farmers stopped coming to my father's mill. They became afraid. The Jews began to run away from the village, wherever their legs could carry them. They went to the woods and to other villages and to certain Gentiles. My mother was frightened and wanted to leave, too, but Papa said no, how could we live in the forests? My sister, Batya, was just nine."

One day when he had gone for his music lesson, the Germans came. They set fire to every Jewish house in the village and to his father's mill.

"When I got home I found everything in ruins, and my parents and Batya were dead." The boy's voice was remarkably steady, only his eyes betraying his grief. "I sat with them a long time, until a neighbor came. She brought me bread and milk, and she told me to hide myself in the forest and never to come back. She said, 'Go to the partisans. Don't use your Jewish name.' She told me to be a good boy and she crossed herself. When I ran to the forest, she called after me, 'God of mercy be with you.' God!" His voice was bitter. "I didn't even know what 'partisans' meant. I just knew she was trying to help me."

There was a silence.

"As another farmer did," Mottele went on. "I took care of his sheep. I think he guessed I was Jewish. He said, 'Find this Diadia —Uncle Misha. He'll take good care of you. Find him. Don't trust the others!'"

"He told you right."

"But that's not what I want, someone to take care of me!" Mottele cried savagely. The mask was completely dropped now from the boy's face and voice, and he spoke as demandingly as any powerfully motivated grown-up partisan. "I want to fight, like you and Lyonka! I know the forest now! I know animals—forest animals and human animals! I must fight, Diadia Misha!"

"There are many ways to fight, Mottele," Diadia Misha said evenly.

"That quiet kid, like a *shaygetz* with his fair hair!" said Lyonka with a laugh. He and Sarah sat smoking cigarettes and drinking coffee in the *budke*, the night after the boy had revealed himself to Misha and Lyonka. "Before he told his story, I could swear he had no feelings. But God, Sarah, he's really so violent inside, I thought he'd explode!"

"So all right. At last he was able to let a bit out," said Sarah dryly.

She stirred restlessly, as memories tormented her. She could have guessed at Mottele's story; it wasn't new to any of them in camp. Everyone here had lost people they had loved, or were, like the boy and herself, sole survivors of their families. Diadia Misha had told them not to hold on to the past. Nothing was to matter, he warned sternly; just the order of the day, the mission, the strength to fight and survive and destroy . . . and destroy. But Mottele, so young and vulnerable, was too much a reminder and symbol of the recent past!

Sarah struggled to retain her self-discipline as she listened to Lyonka.

"So Mottele's one of us," she said.

"It's time you let a bit out, too, Sarah," said Lyonka. He tried to take her hand, but she made a face and pulled away.

"I let out what I like," she said harshly.

She stood up. "The men brought back four wounded, and we're low on antiseptics and bandages."

"All right."

"It's not all right. We need a lot of things."

"Just things, is it, Sarah?"

"Just things."

"I'll see you get them tomorrow. Give me a list," said Lyonka as he got up. He was familiar with Sarah's moods by now; this one could lead to arguments, and he preferred to have some quiet time before the mission next day. "We're going to Ovruch. Sergei's there already, got himself a room inside the town. He sent word that a group of policemen want to defect and join us. They'll bring weapons out, ammunition, anything else we ask for."

"I need all the medicines they can get, and antiseptics. . . ."

"Tomorrow's a Russian holiday, so people will be allowed to go in and out of town without permits. Misha's sending some of us to see what's going on exactly, how many soldiers are camping there, which way they're heading and so on."

"Clean bandages and . . . and vodka. My sick ones need vodka."

"All right—vodka," said Lyonka. "Mottele's coming with us."

"No!"

"But it's perfect! A young boy, you know, innocent, a Ukrainian, in rags and begging like the other beggars at the church. Mottele can tell us a lot just by mixing with the others, one of the bunch, watching everything."

"It's too *soon* to send him out. The boy needs training."

"He can be very useful already."

"No, Lyonka, it's wrong. It's crazy!"

"Why? He'll take his fiddle, and he'll be playing all their

favorite songs, and he'll sing, fiddle away. . . ."
"It's too soon to use him!"
"Mottele's absolutely perfect for this job."
"Forget it, Lyonka! He's only a—"
"Partisan, like us," Lyonka put in roughly.

2

Diadia Misha had decided on sending Mottele with his son and the other partisans to Ovruch almost before the boy had finished telling his story. What a break for the mission, Diadia thought.

The boy looked "Aryan," he behaved like a natural Ukrainian peasant or beggar, he could play his violin, beg for coins, be innocence itself while observing the whole drama from a box seat, as it were. The boy and his fiddle could perform a real *mitzva* for the partisans in this way. Actually Diadia would have preferred to keep the boy in the "family camp" nearby, for mothers and children, and some sick old people; the children in particular needed help with chores and tutoring, for Misha was anxious to keep up their Hebrew studies, if only to divert them from the hardships of camp.

But he thought Mottele would certainly have rebelled at that idea. After revealing himself, he had asked, as audaciously as any grownup, to be active against the Nazis. And indeed Misha had crucial need of the boy's talents. He was amazed at the way Mottele could handle his emotions at age twelve, and he was impressed by the boy's shrewdness. The Lord Himself knew how he'd managed to hold on to his precious violin, yet he *had* managed, despite the months of terror and flight and forest living, concealing it, protecting it, clinging to it. It was more than a fiddle, of course; it was his family, and Diadia Misha understood that better than most. His saving the fiddle, Diadia reflected, took inventiveness as well as stubbornness—and that quality had its military uses. Mottele and his fiddle would go to Ovruch.

In his diary before that mission, Diadia Misha wrote:

Our camp in those days was located among the thick woods around the town Ovruch. In each of the villages in the neighborhood we had sources or spies who were informing us of the mood of the German occupying army, and also the civilian population. One day our spy in Ovruch informed us of a big group of policemen who wanted to join us. . . .

I decided to take this opportunity to send to Ovruch a few of my people and find out the number of soldiers and military camping there. . . .

Among others, I sent Mottele, who was to inform me immediately, through our connection in Ovruch, if anything happened to them. . . . Just in case, I supplied him with an identity card under the name of Dmitri Robena, son of Ivan Robena; if necessary, he was to say he was going to search for his father, who was in a camp of Russian prisoners of war. The identity card was stamped very artistically by one of the partisans, who was a professional stampmaker.

Mottele was very excited when Diadia Misha told him. "And what about a gun, Uncle Misha?"

"Forget the heroics," Diadia Misha said sharply.

"But Lyonka—"

"*You're* going as a Ukrainian beggar. We're about to dress you in rags again. You're going to the biggest church in Ovruch, which Lyonka will show you, and you'll sit outside there with the rest of the beggars. You'll play your violin and you'll sing their songs. But mostly you'll be looking at everything and memorizing everything of importance to relay to me later on."

They were in the *budke,* surrounded by the men of the mission, who were helping themselves to steaming mugs of coffee which Sarah was filling. The boy felt all their eyes on him as he sucked in his breath, swallowed his disappointment and asked cheekily, to hide his feelings, "How will I know what's important to you?"

"Everything and everyone that's German!"

Misha handed Mottele his forged identity papers. Then he rehearsed the boy on what he must say, in Ukrainian, to any German or local person who might test his presence.

Mottele dressed himself according to Misha's orders: torn shirt, ragged shorts, torn cap, no shoes. He carried his violin in its case.

"Take care of yourself, Mottele," Sarah burst out as she ran from the *budke*.

"I think Sarah's in love with you, Mottele," Lyonka teased the boy, to the delight of the men.

Mottele blushed. "You shouldn't say things like that, Lyonka."

Four of them were going: Lyonka, two brothers called Tad and Volodya, and Mottele. In the late afternoon they were to rendezvous at the small flat of Sergei on the outskirts of Ovruch, there to organize the defecting policemen into groups of twos and threes for their escape to the forest partisans.

The town of Ovruch was special to Jews, and everyone in the mission knew just how special. Before Hitler, that medieval town in Zhitomir oblast had always had Jews, in particular the ultra-orthodox Hasids, large numbers of whom had served as rabbis into the nineteenth century. Since the Russian Revolution, Ukrainians had not exactly been inactive; they had initiated many pogroms, yet Jews had persisted in Ovruch, and half the population remained Jewish until 1941, when the Nazis overran the town. Only a few Jews escaped to the woods; all the rest were killed. Now the town was a crucial way station for the Germans to the Russian front.

The men and Mottele entered the town by separate routes. Mottele had been told that the church was the tallest structure in Ovruch, and he headed straight for it. He could see farmers already gathering in the square, which was close by. They wore their holiday finery, and they stood around talking in groups or promenaded with their families. Mottele concentrated his attention on the long path leading up to the church door. On either side of the path there was a row of beggars and cripples of all ages, their caps on the ground before them, singing holy songs and asking for alms.

Mottele didn't want to part with his cap, so he bought a small bowl at a market stall, then took the last place in one row of beggars, nearest to the square and the promenaders. He sat cross-legged on the ground, put the bowl between his thighs and brought out his violin. His heart was racing. He looked around furtively as he picked up the bow, crooked his arm for the fiddle, drew the bow across, turned a peg to adjust the pitch, all the time desperately hoping for a glimpse of his comrades, but to no avail. He hadn't been inside a town since he had fled his own, and he was frightened. He felt terribly alone, isolated and exposed in enemy territory, and he began to tremble with sudden fear of discovery. He was aware that some farm lads had drawn near, expectant and tittering, and he looked up at them at last, forcing himself to remember Misha's admonition: "Don't think. Do your job, and report back!"

Softly at first, as though to test his nerve, he began to sing a Ukrainian song, without accompaniment. He had often stood near the church in his native village, listening to the folk songs of the beggars. Now, in his thin soprano, he deliberately chose one that the farm lads probably knew, the popular folk song about the ant. The ant, the song went, was complaining to God about her bitter luck:

I am the most industrious of animals, but I am always exposed to danger.
Everyone tramples me with his feet, and I cannot defend myself.
Therefore, I ask of God at least one pair of wings!

Some of the lads recognized the song and joined in on the last line, then Mottele played it, in a livelier tempo, on his violin. He got a nice round of applause at the finish, and he started another song, and now people began to wander over from the square toward him. Someone called out his favorite, and Mottele promptly played it. The crowd grew bigger around Mottele, to the chagrin of the professional beggars. His fiddle playing and singing were clearly more attractive than their blandishments. The farmers started to throw coins into Mottele's bowl and some girls stuck biscuits in the rucksack hanging on his shoulder.

Mottele's confidence was growing. He smiled at the crowd, nodding his thanks to this one and that one, remembering to look around him for anything that looked German. All farmers and kids, and nothing important that I can see to memorize for Diadia Misha, he was thinking, when chaos struck the crowd. Mottele saw that the people were pushing at one another, making a path for someone to come through to him. It was a German officer, accompanied by a young German nurse, in white from cap to shoes.

Mottele had never seen a uniformed German before, and he was so startled by this sudden commanding view of the vague specter of his nightmare that his hand stopped its playing in midair. Only momentarily, for whatever happened now, he would have something to report to Misha, and the bowing hand went on playing the song to the end, while the Germans stood waiting. Then Mottele rose and bowed, and he held out his bowl; only he could know about the fear that balled in his stomach. The officer touched Mottele's bowl with his riding crop.

"Come with me," he commanded.

A hush was on the crowd as Mottele put his violin in the case and emptied the coins into his pocket, leaving the bowl on the ground for a beggar to take. He felt the forged papers in his pocket to make sure they were safe. He wondered wildly if Lyonka or any of his comrades had seen this unexpected twist to the drama at the church. He felt helpless and afraid, but somehow he wanted his friends to know that no matter what was in store for him, he would never give them away. White-faced, he followed the Germans silently as the respectful crowd made way for them.

They walked for some blocks until they arrived at a two-story building. Despite his inner turmoil, Mottele found himself counting the many cars, motorcycles and military vehicles parked in the cobbled courtyard. A German guard, his rifle at his side, stood at the building's front entrance, and he gave the group a Hitler salute—right arm rigidly thrust forward—as they went inside. Mottele followed the others up one flight, and they came into an immense hall, brightly lit and very noisy.

At scores of small tables adorned with starched white cloths, vases of field flowers and many bottles and glasses, German officers were drinking, eating, talking, laughing, breaking into songs. Embellishing the festive atmosphere were Ukrainian waitresses, pretty and smiling in their colorful costumes, rushing around to fill the officers' orders. The walls were empty except for one large decoration: a life-size portrait of Adolf Hitler, with the broken cross of the swastika above him.

Mottele's head began to hurt as he stood taking in the spectacle, trying to keep a grip on his feelings. Averting his eyes from the Hitler portrait, he looked to a corner of the room where a brown upright piano was being played by an old man, seated very erect and formally dressed in a black frock coat. He looked old-fashioned and terribly tired.

The German officer, noting the focus of Mottele's attention, nodded his head with a smile as if pleased that he had a bright boy with him. He led Mottele to the piano and said something to the old man in German. The pianist stopped playing and asked Mottele in Russian, "Do you read notes?"

"Yes," replied Mottele.

The old man got out a sheet of music and placed it on the piano, asking the boy to take out his violin. Mottele could have laughed with relief as he saw the music. It was Paderewski's "Minuet."

"For you, Sarah," he thought, as he tuned his fiddle and matched his key to that of the piano, his heart pounding. He began the "Minuet," and the old man listened at first, then began to accompany the boy on the piano. Mottele became aware that the hall had grown quiet. Only the lilting, romantic old melody could be heard, coming from under the boy's nimble fingers. His fair head, bending over his fiddle, contrasted strongly with the pianist's gray head. When the duet stopped, the hall shook with applause and table-thumping.

The German officer beamed at Mottele, evidently delighted

with his find. He told both players to continue, and he joined the German nurse and fellow officers at a nearby table. After a few more pieces, the officer came back to the players. He used the pianist as his translator.

"Tell the boy he can have a job here instead of begging. Two hours every day during lunch, four hours in the evening, from seven to eleven o'clock. He'll be paid, let's say, two marks a day, and get his lunch and dinner. Well?"

The pianist translated the German, and added with a warm smile, "And you'll gladden an old man's heart."

The offer shocked and upset Mottele. He had been planning a getaway, concentrating meanwhile on certain officers' uniforms to describe later to Misha, rehearsing over and over in his mind the numbers and types of vehicles in the courtyard, telling himself fiercely that whatever happened, he'd never betray the *haverim*, his comrades. Instead of which, he was being offered a job by the enemy. He stalled for time. Then he said, in Russian, affecting a small boy's whine, "I can't decide what to do. Tell him I was only begging to get money so I could go to Zhitomir and find my father. He's a prisoner of war there, I think. And I have a sick mother at home with three babies to take care of, and I'm their only support."

The old man translated. The officer waved it aside. Mottele hardly needed to hear the old man's wavering translation to understand that the German was dismissing his excuses.

"I'll write to the commandant of Zhitomir about the boy's father. And if he's there, I'll arrange for his transfer to Ovruch prison. Both of you, continue with the entertainment. Ask the boy where he learned to play like that."

"With my uncle," Mottele told the piano player, who translated. "I have an uncle who can play every instrument in the orchestra." Misha would appreciate that one. . . .

The officer smiled and reached out to pat Mottele's head, but the boy instinctively twisted away; and then, to cover his action, which had caused the man's smile to fade, he leaned over and began to rummage in his violin case. He rummaged until he found the mute and, taking his time, studying, mainly for the officer's benefit, the little wooden device that softened vibrations, he placed it on the bridge of his fiddle and stood up. Then Mottele said something to the pianist, and they began to play a Russian love song. The officer stared thoughtfully at Mottele but, seemingly satisfied, he returned to his table.

The compass of the mission had shifted, Mottele thought as he played the music, but he felt that Diadia Misha would be just as pleased. This place was full of Germans of apparently high rank, so what better post for an innocent beggar boy who was also a partisan?

But Sergei and Lyonka and the others had to be informed. He desperately wanted to rejoin them now, but the old man said Mottele would have to stay for his dinner, which was taken downstairs in the kitchen, and come back up after dinner to play the seven-to-eleven-o'clock shift. Mottele had to agree.

Late that night, when Mottele finally was free to leave, he found Sergei, a tall, loose-limbed, freckle-faced man in a Russian greatcoat and peaked cap, waiting for him at the church. Without a word, the man led the boy through many dark alleys to his small flat at the edge of town.

"I saw you go into the German officers' club," Sergei said when they were inside. "My God, what happened in there?"

"It's kind of crazy," said Mottele. "Where are Lyonka and the others?"

"They finished taking the policemen to the camp over an hour ago. We've all been worrying about you!" Sergei exclaimed. "Tell me what happened!"

"Like I said, kind of crazy."

"Take your time, but hurry up!"

Mottele laughed and sat down gratefully in a heavy oak rocker, feeling safe and unthreatened at last.

"Want something hot, boy, some coffee?"

"What, no vodka, no cognac, after all that schnapps with the Germans!" Mottele joked.

Sergei threw his cap in the air and roared with laughter. Then Mottele told him the day's events, his mood now serious as he tried to remember every detail of the strange occurrences, from the moment of the officer's appearance at the church to his own departure from the officers' club. Sergei looked incredulous.

"And in the bargain, I'm to be paid in German marks," Mottele wound up. Sergei shook his head in admiration.

"And that's only your first mission," he said.

Mottele told Sergei to relay to Misha what he had memorized about the officers' uniforms and apparent ranks, the units, the vehicles, the number of guns and rifles he had managed to see, and as Sergei took notes, Mottele asked him to get "further instructions about my job here." The boy's request was as crisp as any regular partisan's. Sergei reached out and patted him on the back, his freckled face reflecting deep respect.

"A real *mensch,*" he said.

Diadia Misha ordered Mottele to stay on at the club.

He was to be careful, to keep his eyes and ears open, and through Sergei, with whom he was to live, to continue to relay to Misha all developments, not only in the officers' club but in the town. The club, Misha said, was one of many such places that the Germans had opened on the roads to the front, where, with good food, good wine and obliging waitresses, they expected to bolster German troop morale. Misha added that he didn't want the boy taking too many chances. "Dead heroes are no use to me," he warned sternly, and then softened the tone of his message with a *"Mazel tov."*

Sergei told the boy he had better learn to play the one Nazi party marching song that would be expected of all musicians—the *Horst Wessel lied*—and he gave Mottele the words:

> For the last time now has the call been sounded,
> And for the fight now stand we firm and sure;
> Soon Hitler's flag will wave in every street, fast grounded,
> And slavery no longer will endure!

"The pianist will teach you the bloody tune," Sergei said.

But Mottele could not move at once on that, for the next day, when he arrived at the officers" club, the old pianist—"You can call me Uncle Georgi"—said he had orders to take Mottele to the Bureau of the Town Commander immediately. The boy's fears returned.

In the crowded street, he looked around feverishly for Sergei, slowing his walk, holding his violin case on his head in hopes that Sergei could single him out and follow him if he was near, but that was in vain.

Inside the old town hall, now guarded by German soldiers, Mottele was taken to the commander, a trim, erect man with a Hitler mustache. He was told that his rags and bare feet were hardly suitable for the officers' club; the commander had ordered his tailor to come and fit the boy for a proper uniform of a German soldier, also a beret of the same material. The commander, a Ukrainian in German uniform, winked and beamed conspiratorially at Mottele, who began to sweat.

He'd been more than ready to follow Diadia Misha's instructions, eager, proud to be used for the cause, but this—to be dressed up in the murderers' own uniform, to wear the swastika, to be their duplicate! He very nearly gave in to an elaborate Yiddish curse.

Then the pianist, Georgi, smiling ingratiatingly at the commander, nudged him back into reality. Mottele forced himself to smile, too, and say thank you very much in Russian.

That night, Sergei nearly burst with laughter at the story.

"It can't be for very long, and it's a great joke on them," he told the boy. "You'll see them all in *drehrd* yet. Go ahead—curse them all into hell, but only to me, Mottele, only to me!"

Two days later, when Mottele arrived in the kitchen for his lunch, a package addressed to him was on the table near his plate of fried sausage and potatoes. The cook, an immense Ukrainian who seemed to live in his stiff white uniform, was amazed to see the military uniform that Mottele lifted from the package. The cook liked the quiet, well-mannered boy, who would always play his favorite song, "Rose-Marie," whenever he asked, but now he snorted as Mottele got into the uniform and beret and boots.

"Be sure and wear that on the street, too, you little Nazi," the cook said in disgust.

"I mean to," said Mottele.

And when Mottele went to play, dressed up in his new soldier uniform, everyone in the hall stopped what he was doing and applauded.

It was always late at night when the young partisan made his way back to Sergei's flat after the evening's entertainment. The owner of the house where Sergei lived was a stout, good-natured Ukrainian woman with no husband and several children, and Mottele hoped that if the commander or the German officer who first spied him tried to check on him, they would assume she was his mother. But no one bothered him or Sergei in their hideout. Mottele didn't know German, but some German sounded like Yiddish, so he could occasionally eavesdrop on soldiers who had been at the front. Each day he reported to Sergei on the numbers of men and vehicles, and the comings and goings inside the club.

In his free time, between his playing hours, he walked around the town, reading and memorizing the placards on the small shops—mostly printed in Ukrainian or Russian—and the notices posted at the police station. He saw one big WANTED sign that carried the names of a dozen policemen who had "defected to the bandits" in the forest. A price was on each of their heads, because they had also "stolen pistols, rifles, ammunition and medicines" when they fled. A crowd had gathered before that WANTED sign, studying it, keeping their thoughts to themselves. Mottele heard not a word against the defectors.

There was one area, next to the kitchen where Mottele took his meals, that from the first had aroused the boy's curiosity. This was a long, dimly lit corridor which appeared to have storage rooms on each side. The cook occasionally used one room, leaving that door open for his convenience; all the rest were closed and probably locked. One evening after his dinner, and after the cook had gone home, Mottele stole into the open storage room.

He found himself in a cellar filled with empty crates, barrels of herrings and other, empty barrels, possibly for use in carting away the club's garbage. He shrugged, and was about to leave when his attention was suddenly riveted on the wall opposite the entrance to the room: it had a deep, long crack in it, evidently from a bombing. Mottele went to it, running his hand over the fissure, poking his fingers inside and loosening some small stones.

"What if," he asked Sergei that night, "explosives could be stuck inside that crack, say enough to blow up the whole officers' club?"

Sergei stared at the boy. "Well, that's quite a thought. I'll ask Diadia Misha. Let's see what he thinks."

And in his diary, Diadia Misha wrote exactly:

I liked the idea. I delegated Popov, our mine manufacturer, as we called him, to meet with Mottele and find out the precise details.

Lift up thy voice with strength;
Lift it up, be not afraid . . .

ISAIAH 40:9

3

Only Sarah, her eyes dark with fear and anger, objected. Strongly.

"Enough is enough!" she said. "The burden on Mottele is already too big. He's just a child."

"He left childhood behind a long time ago," Diadia Misha said.

"Let Popov do the whole thing," she argued. "He and Sergei are the experts. They're used to this kind of sabotage, they know their way around, and the risks. Lyonka," she pleaded, "tell Diadia Misha not to use Mottele for this!"

"But Mottele is the only one in a good position to get the explosives inside the club," said Lyonka.

"We have lost enough children!"

"I'm worried, too, but he's *the only one—*"

"Misha, I beg you, Misha!" Sarah stormed.

"Mottele wouldn't like you to beg for him," Misha replied coldly.

The next days were learning days for Mottele.

Since it was harvest time, farmers' carts were allowed to go in and out of town freely to gather their harvest of wheat and barley and sugar beets. Sergei became one of the farmers. He got himself a cart and filled it up with straw sheaves used for binding hay into bundles, and he joined the farmers riding out to the fields. German guards on the bridge waved him over. Concealed underneath the sheaves lay Mottele, traveling to his appointed place to meet Popov. Sergei kept driving the cart horse until they reached the edge of a field some kilometers from Ovruch. Popov was waiting.

They wasted no time getting down to business, for Mottele had to be back at the club for his lunch and the entertainment. The boy described the storage room, and detailed for Popov the depth of the crack and the texture of the wall. Popov listened intently, and he speculated that the crack would have to be widened by loosening the stones inside it—which Mottele had already tried—in order to admit *tal*—the explosive. He estimated that the sabotage action, to be effective, would need at least eighteen kilograms of *tal;* and he figured the distance that Mottele would have to run from the area, after lighting the fuse, to be safe.

"That's a hell of a lot of explosive for you to get into that place," Popov said.

"We can do it," said Mottele.

"You mean *you* can?"

"That's what I mean."

Popov went back to Misha with his estimates, and Sergei, Mottele and the cart of straw headed for Ovruch. Inside town, Mottele got out of the straw and into his uniform, and then he walked to the officers' club in time for lunch.

Inwardly, he was nearly sick with the excitement of the morning and his secret mission. It was hard not to show his feelings, but he'd lived in hiding long enough to know how to mask them; and also, these days, he could concentrate on his fiddle. Mottele appeared very upright and handsome in his uniform. He looked straight at the German officers and got them on their feet as he opened up smartly with the *Horst Wessel* song followed by *Deutschland Über Alles.* He liked getting them all up on their feet: he could count heads better that way than while they were sitting stuffing themselves at the tables.

"You look very happy today," said Uncle Georgi. "That was good, very lively!"

"Thank you—*vielen Dank,*" Mottele said, using the German phrase, which he had learned, to amuse the pianist whom he was fond of, but also for the benefit of any officer within earshot. From here on, he had decided, he would be as obliging and as ingratiating as . . . as the waitresses or this old man, until the job was over. He was in the middle of a sentimental love song when he suddenly figured out how to get the explosive into the club.

Sergei thought the idea was perfect: When Mottele left the club at night, he would leave his violin somewhere in the club and just bring out its wooden case. The case would become the means for transporting the blocks of explosive to the cellar. It was risky, said Sergei, but so was the whole plan.

Late that night, as Mottele left the kitchen, he hurried inside the storage room, hid his violin inside an empty herring barrel, closed his empty case and took it home with him. Next day, when he arrived at the club for his lunch, he carried the first three kilograms of *tal* inside his case. He went directly to the kitchen, being careful to follow his usual routine, and ate his lunch. But he dawdled, stalling for time until the cook, who hated to see the boy in his Nazi uniform, left the kitchen to go out for some fresh air or a smoke. Then, swiftly, the boy entered the storage room, took out the explosive, stuck it in the crack, transferred his violin from the barrel to its case, and went back to the kitchen table to finish eating before going up to the hall to play.

In this way, within several days Mottele managed to transport all eighteen kilograms of the explosive into the officers' club. Each night, before he left the storage room, he extracted a few more stones from the crack to make room for the next day's haul, and by the sixth day, Mottele had pushed the last of the *tal* into the deepened crack. He camouflaged the wick, which extended from the wall at floor level, with dirt, stepped back to survey his handiwork, and nodded his satisfaction. All that now remained was Diadia Misha's word to light the wick.

There were, to be sure, one or two remonstrances from Uncle Georgi during this period.

"You seem to be eating herrings off your violin these days," the old pianist told Mottele, holding his nose.

"It's the new varnish I've been using," the boy said. "I'll stop it."

The waiting seemed endless, but the moment, Mottele was warned, had to be exactly right to make the Germans pay the fullest price on this mission.

"And for my own vengeance," Mottele told Sergei to relay back to the partisans.

"That especially," Sergei agreed.

Whenever he could, Sergei now took Mottele on trial runs. They walked casually through the main street and through back alleys, and Sergei drew sketches of the terrain, covering the best and alternate ways leading from the club to the lake. They went to the lake several times, making a pretense of fishing, but searching for a shallow area over which Mottele and his precious fiddle could eventually cross safely; for on the other side, partisans would be waiting for him.

And then Sergei reported solemnly that Diadia Misha had decided to leave the moment of the explosion to Mottele himself. Sergei, watching the boy's reaction to this, saw Mottele's eyes gleam with pride at his commander's confidence.

"He was right to leave the timing to me," the boy said calmly.

"*Chutzpah* yet!" said Sergei, who tried to make a joke of it. He loved this audacious boy, who was being asked to do a man's work and might not come out of it alive.

Mottele waited, and he chose deliberately: the day that a group of high-ranking officers were expected at the club. A whole division was on its way to the Russian front, he learned, to rescue the situation after severe blows suffered by the German Army. The rumors were all over town. The division had been transferred from railway cars to trucks, because too many trains were being blown up by partisans. The new German division was coming by way of Ovruch, and the officers wanted some respite in the town before pushing on.

Mottele sent the agreed-upon code expression to Diadia Misha: "*Gut Yontiff.*"

Before Sergei left with the greeting, dressed in his greatcoat, with his few belongings in his rucksack, he clasped Mottele to him with unexpected emotion. But Mottele pushed him away.

"It's got to be just another day," Mottele said.

"You're right. Good boy."

They shook hands.

On his way to the officers' club with his violin, Mottele nodded to this man and that man whom he'd come to recognize during the past few weeks. His heart raced with such a fearful expectation that he wondered if they, too, could hear the pounding. Some tipped their caps in deference to his German uniform. Others looked stonily ahead—because of his uniform, he speculated. Mottele swung along, hoping that he reflected the festive mood of the small town. As he passed the armed guard at the club's entrance, he noticed that more vehicles and motorcycles than ever were arriving in the courtyard.

By four o'clock the big hall seemed to be rocking with the growing hilarity and commotion. Officers, talking loudly, eating, clinking glasses and beer mugs, toasted one another, burst into song, trying to make the hall, it would seem, into some noisy Bavarian rathskeller. The waitresses had fresh coiffures and starched aprons, and the buffet table seemed about to collapse under the weight of the food and beer and cognac bottles. Soldiers at some tables were already drunk, and singing. Pianist and fiddler could hardly make themselves heard above the commotion.

The old pianist looked tired out from repeating Strauss waltzes by request; but Mottele didn't mind the repetition—in fact, it freed his mind to concentrate on the task ahead, and acted as an emotional safety valve. For he felt the tension and fever growing in his head and stomach, and struggled to remain steady. He had a sudden new problem: the cook had told him he was staying on late to serve the larger number of men, and Mottele wanted to be sure that both cook and pianist were safely out of the club before his final action. They were his friends.

With only short pauses, the players kept at the music. Over his violin, Mottele stared through the smoky haze at the red, high-spirited faces of the officers. More and more of them were getting drunk. From time to time an officer came over and asked for "his" song and one drunken soldier suddenly screamed in a savage voice, "Violin, play 'Volga, Volga'!" Another officer stood up at his table, embraced a bottle of cognac and sobbed out snatches of a sentimental hit song: "My father won't recognize me, my mother doesn't love me, and I don't want to die, I'm young!" This was greeted with jeers and roars of laughter, as a fellow officer uneasily pulled him to his seat.

The pianist translated the German for Mottele. My father wouldn't recognize me either, Mottele thought bitterly as he played. Go on—rejoice, drink, get drunk. . . . I have one big song coming up which will really tear you to pieces!

At eleven o'clock, the pianist said he was leaving for home, but that Mottele should go to the kitchen for some late supper.

"It's been a hard day," the old man said. "I asked cook to save you something hot before you leave."

"Thank you, Uncle Georgi."

An officer took the pianist's place and began a drinking song. Mottele packed up his fiddle, but before he started down to the kitchen he took his last look. Officers were now dancing with the waitresses and with other officers. And the stern picture of Hitler on the wall seemed ridiculously out of place against all the merriment and commotion. God made you, so you're supposed to pass for men, the boy thought. He felt curiously light-headed and the tension twisting his stomach seemed less. Well, let them have their fun. . . . Now to get to work!

The cook had put Mottele's supper on the table. The boy told him he was too tired to eat anything much, but he nibbled on some bread and pushed the food around.

"See you tomorrow," said Mottele.

He waited until the cook left, and gave him an extra five minutes to clear the courtyard.

Then Mottele picked up his violin and went to the storage room.

The darkness closed him in, but Mottele knew every inch of the place by heart. Moving quickly to the crack in the wall, he brushed away the dirt that camouflaged the wick and pulled it out to its full length, then lit the end. He felt completely detached, as cold as the wall he touched. He and Sergei had figured that the delayed fuse would give him time to walk, not run, from the place; he should have enough time to get out the front gate before starting to run.

Mottele made it walking deliberately to the armed soldier at the entrance. The boy even decided on a small parting joke. As he passed the guard, he thrust out his right arm and called:

"Heil Hitler!"

The guard burst into good-natured laughter. "Heil Hitler, you little Ukrainian pig!"

Mottele continued walking as far as the gate. Once through it, he began speeding through cobbled streets and back alleys whose twists and turns he had rehearsed with Sergei. He ran in the direction of the lake. And as he ran he listened, straining every nerve for what was surely to come.

He had gone about two hundred yards when the terrible explosion shook the ground under him. The boy stopped and pressed himself against a wall in a state of awful fear and joy. Windows and doors in nearby buildings were being blown out, and soon he could hear the sirens going and policemen's whistles. People were running out of their houses and buildings in all directions, and rockets seemed to be lighting up the whole town.

Mottele waited no longer, and ran on to the lake. He got to the shallow area selected by him and Sergei, and waded out, holding his violin case above his head with both hands. The water came nearly to his neck, and his footing was unsteady, but he managed to keep going, only once turning his head to glance back. He saw the sky above the town lit up with an enormous spreading fire. Then he forgot his fear, and as he waded and stumbled toward the partisans waiting on the other side of the lake, he found himself rejecting Papa's favorite proverb: "One knows a real Jew by his pity." Not by his pity, not anymore, Papa, the boy thought, but by his vengeance!

That was the way he told it later to Diadia Misha, who wrote in his diary about Mottele's revenge:

On the other side, behind a hill, a cart waited for Mottele with the fastest horses that we had in our camp. Five armed partisans sat waiting there, among them Lyonka, Sergei and Popov; ten arms reached out to pull the boy into the cart. The horses galloped away and sped into the forest. Mottele couldn't utter a word at first because of his excitement. But slowly he calmed down. He looked at the red sky, and clenched his fist, and he cried out, "That's for my parents, and for my little sister! Not pity, but vengeance now, Papa!" He was saying it for all of us, this boy, and it was for me—for my parents, for my wife, and my own little daughter, Fanny, who was thirteen.

*If I am not for myself, who will be
for me? And if I am only for myself,
what am I? And if not now—when?*

TALMUD

4

The resourcefulness of this youngest partisan, and the success
of the dangerous mission, awed Diadia Misha and his followers.
All the fighters put their lives on the line with each mission, but
this youngster had needed no indoctrination from the start. He
was, thought Misha, a true, instinctive son of the Maccabees. At
first Misha even thought that the camp should celebrate the
boy's courage, make a fuss, decorate him. But Misha dropped
the idea, for wouldn't each partisan deserve the same? Especially those members of his nucleus of seventeen who, only
months before, had broken out of ghetto Korets to fight with
him in the forest? This camp actually existed because of what
that nucleus had begun.

In their so-called Jew Town of Korets in Volyn, where Jews
had lived for six hundred years, most of the three thousand
Jewish inhabitants, including Misha's wife and daughter, had
been murdered by the Nazis. Yet the little Ukrainian town had
been no primitive Sholom Aleichem *shtetl* of deprived Jews;
their Gentile neighbors and farmers had in general been
friendly, and many could speak Yiddish as well as their own
language. When—how—did they develop their abnormal at-
traction to corpses? When did necrophilia start taking over
their minds and hearts?

In that town of his youth, with its pretty river and turreted
castle fortress, Misha had been a civic leader, was chairman of
the Jewish Artisans Union, had served on important committees
like the Free Loan Society and the Popular Cooperative Bank.

Jews in the town outnumbered the Gentiles by two to one and owned all the best houses, shops and factories, the Poles and Ukrainians being mostly laborers and farmers. Misha had been born Moshe Gildenman. He'd been active in the General Zionist groups, and while he loved his storied town, he dreamed of leading an *aliyah* to Palestine one day. To his gentle, adoring wife, his son, and thirteen-year-old Fanny, he was, not unexpectedly, a *gantser mensch,* a whole man, a born leader, and he was also that to many of his non-Jewish neighbors, who worked in his factory, or whom he trained in the local orchestra.

The real aristocrats of the town had been the "three wise men," as they were affectionately dubbed: the Russian Orthodox priest of the Ukrainians; the Roman Catholic priest of the Poles; and the chief rabbi of the Jews. These elite would meet regularly to discuss social and religious matters, talking over glasses of tea and savory cakes in the town hall, but the Korets rabbi was the most famous of the three. Other important rabbis came great distances to meet the chief rabbi, who was on such good terms with his Gentile counterparts. Not since the czars ruled Russia had there been a pogrom in the little town of Korets.

So it was for the Gildenmans until the year 1941, when, on June 22, the German Army invaded Russia. On that June day, the Russians had just finished an asphalt road which would continue the main artery of Korets to the great cities of Lwow and Kiev, and the townspeople were to have had a ceremony on the bridge over the river at noon. At six o'clock in the morning, the first bombs fell on the marketplace in the center of town, which led the people to joke ruefully, "The Russians have finished the road just in time for the Nazis to use it."

With those bombs, life for the Jews of Korets changed forever.

Overnight they lost their homes and property. Synagogues and factories were burned down, and it was as though a sudden strange sickness infected the Gentiles of Korets, even before the Nazis marched in. After the Nazis came, all the Jews, including the chief rabbi, were herded into houses in a few streets which were enclosed with barbed wire, creating an instant ghetto, and the Nazis decreed two main *Aktions* against the Jews.

The first, a pogrom, began on a big scale on a beautifully mild day. The German and Ukrainian policemen made the Jews turn out and line up, and said they had orders to select "the weak and the useless ones" for some less arduous tasks. The "selection" included all old Jews, mothers and young children. Among the selectees were Moshe's wife and daughter. Some 2,200 Jews were thus marched away under armed guard in the direction of the forest. All the other Jews, threatened with machine guns, were told to return to their jobs and their homes. Already that night, many began to sit the seven days of *shivah* for the dead, for they never expected to see any of the 2,200 again.

The next day, the Nazi guards selected a number of "strong Jews," Moshe Gildenman and his son, Symcha, among them, and led them under guard to the forest, where they could see what the Nazis had done: they had shot everyone. The bodies were piled on top of each other like sacks of flour. The Jewish men were ordered to dig an area wide and deep enough for a mass grave, and some men, who started to claw at the bodies in search of a loved one, were shot to death. The others dug the grave.

In this way, Moshe's son came across the coat that he had thrown around his mother when she and his sister had been led off.

The Gestapo commander of the ghetto barked orders, pointing his gun at the Jews, telling them to dig, and for a brief moment Moshe Gildenman looked his way, taking him in, memorizing the man. He was very blond and handsome, what Hitler liked to call the true Nordic type, sturdy and clean-cut with his narrow oval face, narrow nose, frosty blue eyes that hardly blinked. He flourished a riding crop, which he pointed with one hand, while he held a gun on the Jews with the other.

That night the people gathered at the synagogue, and after the first Kaddish was said, Moshe went on the dais, and he told the gathering: "Listen, unfortunates, doomed to death! When I look at the unflinching face of the Gestapo commander, I wonder whether he is human. If so, then I am ashamed to belong to the human race. When I look at your reaction to this terrible atrocity, committed against us by the Germans and the Ukrainians, I begin to doubt whether we are the descendants of the Maccabees—and I am ashamed! Know that we are *all* doomed to death, sooner or later! But I shall not stretch out my neck to the slaughterers! Before I die I must take vengeance on the Germans, and only then will I die with a clear conscience. We must go to the forest to fight! *Fight!*"

But only a few believed with Gildenman that they could get away. Where could they go, how would they live in the forest? The Korets Jews had no weapons or ammunition, and anyway, the Russians would soon come and liberate their town, wouldn't they? Remember, Korets had had no real trouble before this for a generation. . . . So the reasoning of most went.

For a time the Jews kept working, Moshe himself on menial work, cleaning the Germans' quarters and latrines, blacking their boots. Symcha went with other strong young Jews and some Russian prisoners of war to work in a quarry outside Korets. Only eight hundred Jews were left in the ghetto. But now at night, in secret, Gildenman organized those who sought to escape with him—sadly enough a small group—for a second *Aktion* was rumored; this one was certain, he felt, to finish off all the Jews, before the SS moved on to the Russian front.

Moshe found a Pole who was willing to sell him a pistol for many rubles, and Symcha started a friendship with a Ukrainian guard who lived near the quarry. The guard was a known thief who might do anything for money, but he seemed willing to talk to Symcha in secret. He said he hated the Germans, and told Symcha, "If you run, take your father and run to my house."

"He probably can't be trusted," Moshe said when Symcha reported the incident. "Lots of Ukrainians tell the Jews to run to them, then they take the money and kill the Jews. But at least this one has a house to run to, and I have a pistol."

Already fear of the second *Aktion* had thrown many Jews into a panic; they took their remaining relatives and fled from the ghetto, and the Nazis shot them to death. Moshe's group counted on one escape route—through a little-known underground tunnel of the old castle which led to the river, across the river to the garden of the Catholic church, near which stood the Ukrainian's house and the forest. Meantime, Moshe held his group together with an iron hand. They wore the yellow Star of David on their armbands and jackets, and they worked without complaining for the hated enemy and took the blows and degradation without defending themselves or replying. And one morning and afternoon, Moshe's little band, which now numbered fifteen men and two young women, slipped out of the ghetto by twos and threes, and took the castle route. Moshe and Symcha were the first to arrive at the rendezvous. Moshe put his pistol to the Ukrainian guard's head and said quietly, "I have a gun at your head. Stay home today."

All day, Moshe's members dashed into safe hiding in the guard's house. Nearby in the quarry, the Germans guarding the Russian prisoners of war and the Jews were unaware that seventeen Jews were a short distance away, on the first leg of their odyssey as partisans. Moshe's group stayed in the guard's house until nightfall. Among them were factory workers, a businessman, a butcher, students and the two cousins Sarah and Jenya, who were hospital helpers. The group ranged in age from Symcha and the girls, who were eighteen, to forty-four-year-old Moshe. Moshe was to remember that the Ukrainian guard didn't act frightened. On the contrary, he seemed to relish the drama under his roof, and actually gave them two loaves of bread, and didn't ask for money, though Moshe gave him some anyway.

"In case someone else should escape, I wanted to leave a friendly Ukrainian behind," he told the others later.

When night came, the little band ran into the forest. All that the members had among them were one pistol and five bullets and the clothes on their backs. They counted on the dense woods to give them some protection, but they needed weapons to survive. And since they had chosen "not to stretch out their necks to the slaughterers . . . but to take vengeance," they would need all their wits to improvise, to be ready psychologically as well as physically to kill or be killed, for not only wolves and wild pigs roamed these woods. They were well aware of such avid Jew-hunters as the Ukrainian Fascists, who supported the Nazis as watchmen in the forests of Poland and the Ukraine.

All Moshe knew was that he and his fellows, pacifists by nature like most Jews, would now have to get used to the act of killing to survive, starting immediately, with that night's improvisation. The first opportunity occurred within minutes of entering the woods. They came on a forest watchman, and led by Moshe they fell on him, attacking without thinking twice, and grabbed his Russian rifle and hunting knife, leaving the man prostrate but not dead.

Astonished with such instant success, they surrounded a Ukrainian guard's house deeper in the forest. Moshe ordered his fellows to "arm" themselves with long branches, holding them like rifles, while he and Symcha burst into the house with their two guns. When the guard reached for his rifle, Moshe grabbed the man's wife and put his pistol at her head.

"I'll kill her unless you give us all your weapons and ammunition," he said. And Moshe realized with a sudden sense of shock that he could really kill the woman, so many lives depended on his action.

The guard looked out the window and saw others brandishing what appeared to be weapons in the dark, and he evidently decided that he was surrounded. He led Moshe to the basement, and Symcha let in the other members, and in this way they captured six more rifles, three pistols, three hand grenades, food stocks and bread. Symcha and the two girls grabbed whatever clothes they could find, including the guard's greatcoat, and Popov decided on a bottle of vodka.

"Must celebrate this victory!" he shouted as they ran back to the forest.

Moshe led the way, running in a zigzag pattern, desperately hoping to throw off any groups roaming around or any Germans to whom the guard might signal. This was January of 1942; the night was clear but freezing. None of the group knew these woods, but all were excited by their daring and success, and all were exhausted. Moshe finally chose a small clearing for their first shelter, working with his companions to scoop out long, wide ditches and camouflage them with leafy branches. When they finished, they stared at their strange booty and at one another. How long would their luck continue?

Popov broke the tension by holding the bottle of vodka aloft and saying, "In the beginning, God said, Let there be vodka," and he got a relieved laugh from the others, but Moshe said, "Put it away, Popov. We'll drink tomorrow. Let's get some rest."

But first Moshe began the age-old prayer, and the new partisans got to their feet as they joined him: *"Borukh atoh adonoi eloheynu, melech ho'olom.* . . . Blessed art Thou, O Lord our God, King of the Universe. We thank thee for our liberation from bondage. . . ."

Next day, Moshe's first command was clear: "Conceal your Jewish identity. We'll take nicknames and be known only by our nicknames, and we'll speak only Russian and Ukrainian when we're not in our camp. We're literally part of the jungle now," he went on, "so we adapt to the law of the jungle. That means kill or be killed."

Yet as he briefed them, he remembered how he felt as he'd held the pistol against the guard's wife, and the sense of shock that flooded him as he knew that he would—could—pull the trigger if necessary. He'd had something of the same feeling when he'd broken into the friendly Ukrainian's house earlier; but he'd felt it more acutely when he held the woman. Was it because of what the Gestapo had done to his own wife and daughter? Could he kill for the sake of killing?

Sarah spoke then.

"We managed it and that's what counts. We're together. I suppose there's a God after all," she said cynically.

Sarah was a tall, lovely, spirited girl with watchful black eyes and curly black hair, whose caustic wit covered her deeply felt emotions. Moshe had known her family well in Korets, and the girl, much sought after, had once had the happiest of dispositions; now she seemed to be drained of all emotion. The first *Aktion* against the Jews had destroyed her parents and grandparents and her young brother. Withdrawn and distrustful, she'd been nevertheless the first to support Moshe's plan for escape, and she had made young Jenya come with them.

Jenya was a sad contrast to Sarah. She seemed far older than her eighteen years, with her brooding pale-blue eyes veiled in her bony face. Her stringy brown hair, now streaked with gray, hung to her shoulders, as dry as straw. Unlike Sarah, her cousin, she had gone wild when her parents and sisters had been killed. She had broken up everything in their flat, and had torn at her own flesh, trying to kill herself. Only Sarah was able finally to control her, and kept Jenya with her as a hospital helper; she became, in fact, Jenya's lifeline.

"The nickname I've selected for myself," Moshe now said, "is Diadia Misha—Uncle Misha."

Smiles of approval lit up the tired faces.

"That's a good Russian handle," Popov said with a laugh. "Well, I won't have to adopt another name myself, will I? Popov's a nickname I've been stuck with since birth!"

"Suits you fine," said Moshe.

"I'll be . . . Lyonka," said Symcha. "What about you, Sarah?"

"I like my name. I'll think it over," she replied curtly.

She stared down, then turned away from the tough, broad-shouldered young replica of his father. Symcha's thoughtful eyes were always seeking hers and she drew away from the contact. In the old days back in Korets, her parents would probably have called it a good match, and the *shadkhen*, or matchmaker, would have been busy with the arithmetic of dowry and qualifications. That was how it might have been. Now they might all be dead tonight or tomorrow. The girl struggled to keep a coldly critical attitude toward Symcha or anyone who might be having ideas. All she knew was that she didn't want anyone to touch her, emotionally or physically. But she felt she understood Diadia Misha fully: she was ready to kill, and that was all she was ready for.

The new partisans got their first real assignment within twenty-four hours, and their first machine gun.

Misha had sent a three-man detail to scout the area near camp, and they had raced back to report that some German and Ukrainian policemen were heading for a nearby bridge, driving a dozen cows before them.

"So we'll let the bastards deliver our rations first, then get to them," Misha said.

He selected his son, and Popov, and the butcher, Josef, to go with him, arming each with a pistol, and himself with the grenades. They ran to the bridge, which proved to be small and wooden, above a reedy marsh. Misha, with his engineering skill, and Popov, who knew a thing or two about bombs, decided between them that the job would need their three grenades. Misha hated to use them up, but perhaps they'd get some other military loot in exchange. He waited until the cows were over, which put the policemen in the middle of the bridge, then he and Popov threw the grenades with precision. They watched them work, the bridge shattering nicely, without too much clatter or fire-eating as it blew up, then settled into the marsh below. The frightened cattle ran in every direction. The saboteurs concentrated on the human booty first.

Josef, the butcher, beat the others to a couple of dazed Germans. He used his butcher's knife to slaughter the men; Misha and Popov finished off the others with their pistols. Symcha had not moved, and seemed to be immobilized in the marsh as he watched Josef. Josef had lost his wife and six children in the Korets *Aktion*.

They took back with them a machine gun, several rifles, pistols and ammunition, and four cows, returning to camp in silence, each person leading a cow. Josef held his butcher's knife at his side, and it dripped blood. Symcha walked behind him, sweating with a fever, and back at camp the fever persisted.

"After this, use your gun," Misha told his son quietly. "Follow orders."

"I'm sorry I let you down, Papa."

"All right, but no matter what, use your gun."

"Papa, how did it feel?"

"How did what feel?"

"To kill."

"How should it feel?"

"I have to know."

"I . . . didn't feel anything. I can't be sure that if I met German children I wouldn't kill them. I didn't have to do that, but I feel that I could have, out of vengeance."

"You don't feel anything, then?" the young man persisted. Misha studied his son.

"The problem of killing doesn't arise as a moral question. We're fighting as guerrillas, as partisans, and this comes after we've seen our families, our women and children, killed because they were Jews. The Germans' whole intention is to wipe out the name of Jew, of Israel. We have no choice of, say, surrendering and facing prison. The Germans will kill any partisan, but when it comes to the Jewish partisan, they will use torture first and then kill. So what we do here in the forest, we do as self-defense, for our survival and for our vengeance. And we're not the only ones with this idea," Misha went on. "In many parts of Poland and Russia, prisoners and Jews are escaping into the forest—from labor gangs, from ghettos when they can, from camps. We don't have uniforms, and we're going to have to steal to get military supplies and food and blankets, but we're soldiers all the same."

"No place for conscience, Papa?"

"Conscience?" rasped Misha. He saw his son's face and he tried to contain his impatience. "You mean we should politely ask, Who goes there, friend or foe?"

"I was thinking about Josef, the way he used his knife."

"So that was his choice."

"The gun would have been cleaner."

"Josef probably thought shooting was too clean. He's had his vengeance. Shooting would have let them off too easy. Dead is dead."

"All right, Papa."

The partisans shifted camp many times, Misha ordering the shifts following each attack on police stations to augment their arms stock. Their main source of food supply was the local population; several partisans would enter a village or farmhouse with a show of guns and take food and horses and cattle by force. The hardest problem was with the Germans who might be on their trail after the dramatic raids, so Misha kept shifting camp, and finally decided to move his group to the wooded region of Zhitomir, hoping that eventually he could make contact with the High Command in Moscow. Now, with a fair arsenal, Misha decided that they could risk building a few huts aboveground, and a field kitchen, and a watchtower in the trees. By the time the partisans got to Zhitomir, the news of their exploits had spread and many Jews hiding out in the forest came to join Misha's band. Every Jew was taken in. Each had his own terrible tale to tell.

One man told Misha of several Jews who had been hidden by a friendly peasant; but then his place was visited by a Ukrainian policeman and both peasant and Jews were led away. Another had escaped over the Polish-Russian border from the big Lodz ghetto, where, he told the partisans, "They're burying children alive with adults who've not died yet!"

Another escapee from Lodz ghetto, a haggard, driven man called Jacob, recounted in a haunted voice how he had handed his infant son to a Gentile family "in some village" in Eastern Poland before escaping over the border; he said he had begged them to get the child to his brother in Palestine after the war, if he couldn't come himself to claim him. The man's eyes, large with grief, sought Misha's approval.

"You did right," said Diadia Misha.

"What if they baptize him?"

"*That's* your worry just now? The child's alive! Write down where you left him. Make a map. Lyonka, help Jacob here to detail exactly where he left his son."

Misha's group was growing. But action was hampered as snows of the long winter blanketed the forest, and the tearing winds howled around them like the howling of wolves. The partisans lacked adequate food supplies and warm clothes to survive the bitter cold. Then, from new recruits from Rozvazhev, Misha learned that the warehouses of that town, between Zhitomir and the city of Kiev, were bulging with everything: clothes, blankets, weapons, food, medicines. Mission Rozvazhev was planned.

For three hours late one night, Misha led his partisans on the march until they reached the town just before midnight—a good hour for a surprise attack. At his signal, grenades were tossed into the police station, telephone and telegraph wires were cut, the German garrison rushed. The gendarmerie was housed in an old church. Popov put a couple of mines under the church wall and it exploded, taking most of the gendarmerie with it, but also the lives of four partisans. The "appropriations group" meantime was making a clean sweep of the pharmacy's medicines and soap, and raiding the warehouses, bringing out blankets and clothes and hams and tobacco and French wines.

The real surprise of the night awaited Misha himself and his group of four men. When they burst into the commandant's house, they found officers, flushed with food and drink, seated around a table, listening to a stately blond woman who was singing a Russian love song, all very *gemütlich*. So swift was the partisan attack that the officers were shot dead where they sat, some sliding under the table, others dropping their heads in their plates. That wasn't so astonishing as what followed, Misha told the rest of his comrades later.

"During the action, the woman remained standing in the middle of the room, her eyes expressing more surprise than fear. She stood motionless with the guitar in her hand, like a statue. Only when one of my partisans grabbed her arm and shook her vehemently did she come out of her petrified state and, in a calm voice, say in Russian, 'At last you have come!' "

Though a host should encamp against me,
My heart shall not fear;
Though war should rise up against me,
Even then will I be confident.

PSALM 27:3

5

At the time that young Mottele joined Diadia Misha's partisans, the Korets nucleus of fifteen men and two girls was intact, but Misha now commanded nearly two hundred people. The news of his unit's daring military offensives had spread quickly, and non-Jewish partisans had also been attracted to Misha's ranks. At first Misha had made no secret about wanting to keep his unit all-Jewish, but after a while, and after judging the worth of each new candidate, he had let in a number of non-Jews. "They're insurance for us," he told Lyonka and his group commanders. "We need non-Jews in our intelligence apparatus, especially in the villages."

The number included also Jewish families who had been hiding in the forest and sought sanctuary with Misha, and old and disabled men. A mobile family camp was built for the families, which would shift with the partisans when the fighters had to change camps. On their part, the families prepared meals for the partisans, helped in the sick bay and cared for the cattle.

Mottele might have landed among them, but Misha, early on, had decided that the boy's intelligence, talent and his Nordic looks fitted him for more active assignments with the fighters; it would have been hard to deflect the boy from his quite articulate motivations and zeal; in any case, after the way Mottele acquitted himself on his first mission in Ovruch, all the partisans were glad he was one of them.

All, that is, except Sarah. Tormented by memories, she continued to resist.

"You've seen enough of killing and guns," she told Mottele one afternoon following the Ovruch mission. "Give it a rest now. Anyway, I need help in the family camp and the hospital."

She and Mottele were walking together along the dew-drenched grassy path to the family camp, carrying some clothes and tinned food for a mother and infant who had fled into the camp the night before. The sunshine, shafting the leafy branches of the oaks; the immense calm and peace that had settled on this part of the forest, now turning green after the long harsh winter; the sudden, light-hearted notes of a bird; the act of just walking alone this way with Sarah—all this was to Mottele in such dramatic contrast with the recent weeks of tension in Ovruch that the boy felt both exhilarated and confused.

Ever since Lyonka had joked about Sarah's being in love with him, Mottele had secretly treasured that thought. He'd liked it when she'd asked him for a kiss. He wanted to kiss her again. He wanted her to know that he would do anything in the whole world for her. But he was a fighter, a partisan, like the other partisans, like her; not a child to work in family camps!

"I can't be with the families, Sarah. I *can't* do that," the boy said.

"Of course you can. And you will."

"You know I only take orders from Uncle Misha."

"I'll tell him I need you in the family camp."

"Don't try that, Sarah," said Mottele in a hard tone.

"Don't tell *me* what to do!"

Sarah pushed angrily ahead of him on the path, her figure in rough boy's pants and loose shirt as erect as a young soldier's. But her steps were so small and light and rapid that Mottele felt she could really fly away if she wanted, like the bird whose song followed them. He hurried up to her anxiously.

"You do understand, Sarah."

"What's to understand? You're just a kid!"

"No."

"Oh, you're hopeless!"

"Please don't be angry with me, Sarah."

"You're too stupid to see—"

"I know it's because of your brother."

"It's not that. They ought not to send you."

"I volunteered, you forget."

"How could I forget!"

"So all right, then. I have to fight!"

"There are Magyars not far from camp, and Misha is saying he wants you to see what they're doing."

"I know; I heard."

"Let them send someone *else*—Lyonka, me—I don't care. But you're just a kid!"

"That's the whole *point*, don't you see, Sarah? No one pays any attention to a kid!"

She stopped then, and turned to look at him, and the boy felt his heart leap with the tenderness he saw in her face.

"It's not a game, Mottele."

"I have to fight in my own way."

"Your way! Next thing is a pistol of your own." She was the old, tough-talking Sarah.

"Yes. That's the next thing," he said stubbornly.

The news that a detachment of Magyars, Hungarian Nazi troops, were bivouacked in a village a few kilometers from camp was giving Diadia Misha concern. He had sent Lyonka and most of his able partisans out on missions; the two-score men and women left behind included sick and wounded, and those who could not be spared from their guard duties. Questions about the Magyars plagued Diadia Misha: Were they on their way to the Russian front, or here to reconnoiter the forests for partisans, for Jews? What was their number? How well were they equipped?

Misha had decided to turn again to his youngest partisan, though he hated to send Mottele out so soon after the Ovruch mission. But he felt that the new mission called for the innocent-boy act again.

In response to Misha's summons, the boy now stood before him, wearing the open-necked shirt and casual pants that Sarah had rustled up. Scrubbed clean, his fair hair severely brushed, he looked like the eager schoolboy he really was. There was something about the eyes, though, Misha thought with a pang. Wise, old eyes, sensitive, boring into one. Not a schoolkid's.

"You think you're ready again?" Misha asked.

Before Mottele could reply, Ivan put in swiftly, "Misha, perhaps you'd like *me* to take this one? I speak Hungarian and German as well as Russian."

Ivan was a defector from Ovruch. A hulking gray-haired military figure of a man, Ivan felt that he hated the Germans more than even the Jews did. His sixteen-year-old daughter had taken a German lover, and the girl and his wife had laughed derisively at Ivan's proposal that they join the partisans with him. Rather than kill his daughter's lover, which had been his first ferocious idea, Ivan had chosen to flee with the other Ukrainian policemen defectors.

Mottele fascinated him. He didn't seem Jewish, and the boy had that *chutzpah* that he, Ivan, had always envied in the few Jews he'd known.

"Commander, I know that village," Ivan went on eagerly.

"No!" The retort rang out from Mottele.

"No? You giving orders, Mottele?" asked Misha.

The boy fell silent under the reproof of his commander in chief, but he looked hard at Misha, expectant nevertheless. Misha turned to Ivan.

"Thank you, Ivan, but this mission is tailor-made for Mottele," he said. "They're Magyars, and he won't be expected to know their language. Does anyone? Well, except you!" The two men laughed easily. "I'll have another mission for you, but later."

Misha couldn't say that he didn't trust Ivan yet, nor the other defectors, and that they would have to prove themselves or be shot. But Ivan guessed Misha's meaning. With a nod of understanding, he turned and left.

"Mottele, he admires what you did," said Misha.

The boy blushed. "I can leave at once, Diadia Misha," he said.

"That's my boy."

"Do I take a horse? Put on the German uniform?"

"No, dammit—no uniform, no horse!" But Misha's voice softened as he saw the boy's face drop. "It's not that kind of mission, Mottele. You're a peasant again, a goatherd in rags. You walk."

"All right."

"Get into your short pants, and, I'm sorry, no shoes. Rucksack on your back. And here, take this whip. Now you're a farmer's boy out herding your goats and, let's see, you've lost the cow."

"Yes?"

"If anyone should stop and ask you who you are, what are you going to tell them?"

Mottele thought a moment.

"I'll tell them I come from Kristinovka village. I'm looking for my cow, the one with red patches and a broken right horn. She got away from me and I have to find her, and she seemed to be making for this village."

Misha grinned. "You've convinced me."

"I'll get ready, then."

"I'll go part of the way with you, Mottele."

"All right."

But the boy hesitated. There was something on his mind, and his face looked strained as, in his straightforward way, he sought for the exact words.

"Diadia Misha, I have something to tell you."

"Yes?"

"I've been reading the Bible again."

"So?"

"I stopped for a while."

"A lot of us stopped for a while."

"I stopped loving God."

"You always loved God before?"

"I think so. Yes. But I stopped. He seemed like a joke."

"And now?"

"I'm not sure why, but I've been reading again, the Prophets and the Psalms. I've been concentrating on the chapters on confidence and vengeance."

"That's very sensible."

"I like to read. I was the best reader in my *cheder.*"

"That's a good reminder for me. I've got to get more books and newspapers in here. We're all starving for them."

"I borrowed your Bible from Lyonka," Mottele went on. "The Prophets are very alive to me again!"

Misha nodded, studying the boy and his strange wise old eyes, feeling the pang again that this child would know no childhood. Then, on an impulse, he suddenly quoted from his own school days, booming it out: " 'The Lord revengeth, and is furious!' "

"Furious?" Mottele retorted. "Him? Well, if there is a Lord!"

Misha was noncommittal. "So you find it's a help—Prophets and Psalms?"

"It is—and some other things."

Like an actor going into a well-known part, Mottele got back into his beggar's clothes. Misha led the way for a time through the woods, where sunshine was bouncing off trees onto the trails. He took silent note of his hidden guards, some in the bushes, some inside the densely branched oaks. Before advancing, he gave them his bird-whistle signal, and the guards peered out briefly in acknowledgment. Misha left the boy about a kilometer from his destination. "I want you back in a few hours, Mottele."

"Shalom, Diadia Misha."

"Shalom. And," Misha added deliberately, "God bless!"

"Shalom. I'll be back soon," was the boy's reply. The part about God had better wait; he needed to give that a lot of thought, a lot. . . . If the Lord was furious, well, so was he, and at the Lord Himself!

The village at the edge of these woods was astonishingly like a small cousin to Ovruch: thatched huts on cobblestoned streets, some small yards back and front for chickens, a horse or cow, lots of trees; in fact, there seemed to be more trees than people. The whole village looked deserted and asleep in the sunshine, but the huts were so tightly shuttered that they appeared to be frightened. Then Mottele saw some uniformed Magyars walking in and out of huts; they went in empty-handed, but came out with their helmets filled with eggs and cheese, and disappeared. The boy headed toward the square, where six very large, flat-topped carts stood. Smoke was curling from one of the carts, probably the field kitchen. Under a pear tree close to this cart, and seated on a bench, was a fat, listless soldier, his uniform unbuttoned. He was alone and bored-looking, reading his newspaper.

Mottele hesitated, and waited for the soldier to spot him, and suddenly the man indeed looked up. His face creased with pleasure when he saw the boy, and he motioned to Mottele to come closer. In sign language, he asked the boy if he wanted some bread, and held out a slice, and Mottele nodded and came closer. The soldier, evidently the cook, threw him the slice, and Mottele caught it and wolfed it down, behaving like any hungry boy. He went and sat next to the cook, who cut off a slice of meat, and put it between two more slices of bread, then stuck the sandwich in Mottele's rucksack. Mottele, by now completely the creative actor, caught hold of the cook's hand and kissed it. The cook ruffled Mottele's hair.

The boy's eyes were on the newspaper, which was in German. Even had it been in Chinese, he intended to take it back to camp somehow, so hungry was everyone for news of the outside world. Well into his part, Mottele decided to show his gratitude, and he climbed up one of the huge wheels of the field kitchen. He took hold of the big ladle lying near a pot and began to stir the soup. The Magyar cook had been startled at first, and watched this bit of business dubiously, but then he smiled his tolerance and satisfaction. From the kitchen, while he stirred vigorously, Mottele could see the contents of the other carts: one held a heavy machine gun, partially covered with green cloth, and the other carts were piled with sacks of fodder, each sack bearing a swastika. "Now, let's not overdo this act," Mottele said to himself as he climbed down.

He and the cook were still alone in the square. The cook seemed half asleep from the heat of the stove. He had taken off his holster and belt. They were on the bench beside him, and Mottele's eyes were on the black revolver in the leather holster. The cook was fanning himself with the newspaper, beaming now and then on Mottele and trying to stay awake, but in a moment the paper fell from his hand, his head dropped to his chest and he began to snore.

Mottele waited, with growing anticipation and fear now, knowing what he intended to do provided no one came into the square. He pressed back his fear, looked all around him, then picked up the newspaper, which he used for shield as he reached toward the holster. He stroked the holster and looked at the cook, who was now whistling in his sleep. Then feeling that his blood was running cold, Mottele undid the flap of the holster, took out the revolver, stuffed it into his rucksack with the newspaper, and stole away.

He was shivering as he went, feeling the same sickness that had torn at him in Ovruch, but he fixed his eyes on the horizon, the woods toward which he began to run. All the dexterous strength he'd had when he climbed up in the cart seemed to be flowing out of him, and he tried not to think what would happen to him if he was caught with the cook's revolver. Or any gun.

Yet a bittersweet thought passed through his mind as he now ran with all his might: Who could have guessed that Sarah's prophecy about a pistol would come true so soon?

Mottele was nearly at the end of the village when a Magyar soldier came out of a hut and mounted his horse, dropping his whip just as the boy came by. He beckoned to the boy to pick it up for him. Mottele stopped dead, fearing that the man might shoot him if kept going. He picked up the whip and handed it to the Magyar, and the soldier smiled down at Mottele, and tossed him a cigarette stub, German-made. With a whack at his horse, he rode off into the village.

Weakly Mottele watched him go, then he backed away and began to run into the woods. He didn't stop running for most of the kilometers back to camp.

6

The whole story of the Magyars, as Mottele told it later in the
budke, to Misha and a dozen partisans, themselves just returned from missions, had them shouting with relief and laughter. The boy, Misha noted, had a strange gleam of pride in his
eye, as he held up and admired the black revolver, and said,
"Come on, Lyonka, let's go to the marsh. You can teach me to
shoot!"

Diadia Misha tried to look angry. "Your shooting can wait,
Mottele. Here I send you on a mission to find out how many
Magyars there are and what arms they have, and you steal guns
from sleepy cooks. You haven't given me your report yet!"

The men laughed again.

"Haven't I just made my report?" the boy said with spirit.
"Look—there were the six carts, so we can figure five men to
a cart; that makes thirty soldiers and one extra with the cook.
They have a machine gun, which I told you I saw. In those sacks
is fodder which they must be stealing from the farmers."

"Nu?" Lyonka put in quietly, with a knowing wink at his
father, sharing his pride in the boy's nerve. Lyonka hadn't
laughed with the others. His old friend from school, David of
Korets, had been killed on a sabotage mission that afternoon.
Feeling exhausted and melancholy, Lyonka stared at his father
and the boy, gratified for the momentary lull and his own narrow escape. He marveled at the boy's audacity, and would have
been glad of his company alone somewhere.

"All right, Mottele," Misha said, smiling at him, "but enough for one day. No shooting lesson yet. Get washed and get some sleep."

Mottele put the pistol back in his rucksack. It was obvious to the partisans, perhaps especially to Ivan, who had thoroughly enjoyed the lad's story, that the boy, having his own gun now, considered himself a true partisan.

That same night, Diadia Misha and a group of men, including Ivan, raided the village. They carried rifles, grenades and machine gun, and caught the Magyars unaware. The partisans shot most of them, Mottele's estimate having proved to be correct, and took a lot of booty back to camp, including the Magyars' machine gun. Ivan hitched a horse to the field kitchen near the old pear tree, and rode it back to camp.

"So you're going to teach him to kill. Congratulations," said Sarah. Her tone was contemptuous.

"He has to be able to shoot. Why not?"

"Why not? Do I have to spell it out for you?"

"Do me a favor, Sarah. Just forget it."

Lyonka strode ahead of her, shoving branches aside with his rifle. He was in a dangerous mood. It was a few days after Mottele's brush with the Magyars and the subsequent raid on the village, and he and Sarah had been assigned to temporary guard duty.

Half the men were still away on missions. Lyonka had that afternoon returned from a sabotage mission, which had finally resulted in blowing up the bridge on the Titarov River near Brosilov. Misha's strategy was in support of Soviet troop movements in a village some miles from the Germans waiting near the bridge for the Russians' approach. The mission had been successful in terms of German lives lost, but the battle had raged for two hours, and four partisans had been shot dead, too. It was only a few days since Lyonka had brought David back on his horse, the first of the old Korets nucleus of seventeen escapees to be killed. Now his nerves were rubbed raw, and he felt unutterably empty inside. He sensed that Diadia Misha had sent him on this relief duty with Sarah to help calm him down.

But Sarah was feeling the terrible human losses, too, and because of this she kept needling Lyonka.

"I'm saying you don't have to be the one, Lyonka."

"Mottele prefers me."

"Naturally. He loves you. But you can tell him no, shooting isn't necessary, wait till you're a man."

"Don't talk like a fool, Sarah."

"It's not foolish."

"I don't want to argue the point. He's going into dangerous situations and he wants to be able to defend himself. What's wrong with that?"

"Everything. It's not safe."

"It's *his* decision, and Misha's."

"He shouldn't be going on those missions—"

"Oh, come on, Sarah!"

"Maybe the war will be over soon!"

"It won't."

"It could be over next week."

"It won't be."

"Lyonka, you listen to me! I want you to stay away from Mottele!"

Sarah's voice had risen. She was no longer just chipping away at his defenses; she had become tough, possessive, demanding, and Lyonka stopped, his shoulders sagging. Then he straightened up and turned on her furiously, all his feelings about that day's acts of vengeance and David's death coming to a boil. He grabbed Sarah by the arms and shook her hard.

"Just shut up!" he shouted.

He kept shaking her, his face, flushed and desperate, close to hers, and then tears came, streaming down his face. Sarah sensed the violence of his anger flowing into her arms. She, too, was terribly angry, but she felt herself slipping into an emotion that was far from anger, as they stood alone and she saw the tears and felt the isolation in that part of the forest. The emotion was new, mesmeric, alarming to her in its passion, yet strangely exciting, and she began to reply, not in anger this time, when they both heard a sudden crunching of leaves and branches, and some steps.

Lyonka's arms tightened around her, protectively now. They stood close together in absolute silence, listening hard. Was it a German? Had they led him to their hideout? Had their voices given them away? The steps came nearer. They came from behind Lyonka. Slowly he released Sarah and turned, readying his rifle. Something still hidden from them jumped, and Lyonka shouted in Russian, "Who's there?"

A huge animal—a wild white pig—leaped out of the bushes. It jumped across the trail and raced into the woods on the other side and disappeared.

In his shock Lyonka broke into a sweat. He turned back to Sarah, and they collapsed together on the trail. Lyonka rolled on the ground. He stretched his arms above his head, and, like a great catharsis that was cleansing and healing, the laughter poured out of him, and he laughed until the tears came again.

When, finally, he was quiet he found Sarah beside him, lying on his arm, watching him quietly and not without amusement. Some of his old agony returned. He pulled the girl close and pressed her to him.

"I love you, Sarah," he murmured. "You know I love you!"

He caressed her face and began to caress her breasts. His eyes sought hers with an imploring look.

"No, please."

"Don't close the door on me, Sarah."

"You don't understand!"

"What's to understand? Love me, Sarah."

"Lyonka, we have to go!"

"In a moment. I just want to hold you this way, and kiss you. I want you, Sarah!"

"Lyonka, don't. Please! I'm so afraid!"

"What of? That old pig!"

"You won't laugh?"

"I won't laugh. Don't move away!"

"I'm afraid of the dark."

"The dark? It's not dark, Sarah."

"It will be. It will be again."

She pushed herself away from Lyonka and stood up, brushing herself off and straightening her shirt.

Lyonka stared up at her.

"We have to go, Lyonka."

He got up then, and swung his rifle back in place on his shoulder. He felt drained and resentful, but vaguely touched by the girl's fears. He had sought to reassure her, but he knew he wanted to feel right with her, too, to love her, to possess her. To feel her respond to him.

Miserably, without another word, he led the way to their relief posts.

I am solitary and afflicted.
The troubles of my heart are enlarged . . .
PSALM 25:16, 17

7

Jacob, the man from Lodz ghetto who had left his infant son with the Gentile family, had been seriously ill for days. He had been wounded in the shoulder when he and several others fled the ghetto, first by cart, then by the sewer-and-marsh route; wounded and ill, he had then roamed the forest for weeks. No, he didn't know if he'd been shot by the Gestapo as he fled, or by the Jewish Police, who worked for the Gestapo, and also for "that bastard who rules the ghetto—the one we call Führer Rumkowski!"

"That's a different sort of Mordechai," he had said to Misha and the boy, Mottele, with a small, apologetic smile the night he had fled into Misha's camp. "He's the Jewish head of the Lodz Council—one Mordechai Chaim Rumkowski—appointed by the Germans. Diadia Misha, I must tell you what's happening to the Jews in ghetto Lodz!"

His voice had shaken, and he was obviously heading for a complete collapse.

"Later." Misha had urged.

"You have to know what's happening there! Rumkowski and the Germans have got the Jews sealed off!"

"I want to know it all. But get better first."

Misha ordered Jacob into hospital. Jenya took care of his wound, doing her best to cleanse and dress it. But she could not help him emotionally. He was out of control. Gaunt, tense, half starved and desperate about his son, Ephraim, Jacob developed a high fever. On the hospital cot, he tossed and moaned for days, muttering in his sleep and, in his few waking moments, staring with glazed eyes as though lost in some private hell.

He was constantly thirsty, asking only for water. Jenya tried to force some food into him, but he pushed it away. One of his constant dreams apparently involved the swamps; he muttered that he had to "hold the child up higher, oh, God, higher. . . ." His dreadful nightmares drove him into delirium, and the fever grew worse. He thrashed about on his cot, calling out for "Marya . . . Ephraim . . ." and shouting once, "Goddamn bastard, why do I have to plead with you?"

And once he held Jenya's hand, when she tried to soothe him and get food into him. His grip was hard, as though he was trying to anchor himself to reality, to a fellow being. But he soon slipped back into his dreams.

Sarah told Jenya to stay with the man as much as possible; Misha had said she was to nourish him and get him on his feet again. For her part, Jenya regarded Jacob not as just another disabled Jew, but as a crucially needed replacement; the unit had lost too many fighters, and it had become personal with Jenya: she had grown fed up with death. She stuck with Jacob.

Then, on the fourth day, the fever disappeared as suddenly as it had begun, and Jacob fell into an exhausted, quiet sleep. When he awoke he looked around him, and uttered one word: "Marya?"

"No, it's me, Jenya."

"Of course, my Marya's dead. So is my son."

"Not Ephraim," Jenya said emphatically. "You got him out, and he's safe, remember? Now you've slept enough, Jacob. Misha says you have to eat."

"I did get the boy out," Jacob said. He stared at Jenya, the memories beginning to flood him again.

"He'll be safe where you left him, I'm sure."

"Safe, you say?"

"He's alive!" Jenya cried. "They killed my whole family!"

Jacob studied the girl quietly. Her eyes were wild with her own turmoil, but she remained steady and gentle with him.

"How long have I been like this?"

"Three, four days. You've had a very bad fever."

"In the ghetto, my wife died of typhus."

"You didn't have typhus, Jacob."

"She didn't have it either, but they threw her with the others in the typhus center. I hid Ephraim, though; I denied them that."

"Yes, you did."

"They were taking us to the killing center outside the camp, and some of us got away. I had to get to this Diadia Misha. We'd heard about him in the ghetto."

"Misha wants you to eat and get well; he needs you."

"He's been here?"

"Once or twice."

"Does he know what's going on in Lodz? My God!"

"Misha says to get some food into you before anything. You haven't eaten for days. Now how about noshing on some chopped liver and onion and some latkes?"

Jacob's eyes widened, then they lit up boyishly and he grinned.

"You've really got chopped liver and latkes?" For the moment he was neither accuser nor hunter, but a man with an appetite.

"I wish I had, but we can pretend, can't we?" Jenya said briskly, and she spooned some thick cabbage and bean soup into his mouth.

Sarah, passing near the hospital hut, took in the picture— Jacob apparently on the mend, Jenya relaxed and comfortable for the first time since Korets days. She left them to it.

"Look here, Jenya." Jacob was pointing to a black-bordered paragraph in the newspaper that Mottele had stolen from the Magyar cook. The paper was in German, which Jacob knew. He was waiting with Jenya in the headquarters hut for Diadia Misha and his assignment.

Jacob was still very thin and a bit shaky on his feet, but his big-boned Slavic face was fleshed out, beginning to beard and he seemed, if not strong, at least resilient. He had the slightly

stooped figure of the scholar or yeshiva student. His brown eyes
sometimes narrowed to slits with a sort of Oriental brooding,
but presently they were wide with anticipation of Misha's arrival, and an assignment. Just now he was studying the paragraph with the well-defined black border.

"The German High Command has reprinted here its instructions to the occupied areas," he went on. "They point out that
this was decreed and printed as far back as November 1939, but
it's to be a reminder to everyone of their obligations to the
Germans. Listen, Jenya." Jacob translated tonelessly:

"Decree of Hans Frank, Governor General of the German-Occupied
Territory of Poland: On the Establishment of Jewish Councils. RE-
MINDER! The Jewish Council of Elders is obliged to receive, through
its chairman or his deputy, the orders of German official agencies. The
Council's responsibility will be to see to it that the orders are carried
out completely and accurately. . . ."

"Completely and accurately," Jacob repeated in a bitter tone.
"Well, that's Rumkowski's cup of tea. But even he will remember that back in 1939 the Nazis weren't yet talking about a
'Final Solution' for the Jews. In fact, Jews could still leave Germany and Poland, too, until the war broke out in 1939; without
money or wherewithal, it's true, but they could get out. The
trouble was that for most of us, the Eastern Jews, there was
nowhere to go. No one would take us, and we couldn't even get
to Palestine."

"We felt safe in Korets, until . . ." The girl's voice trembled.

"You have to read this order here in the context of the real
history, then and now, in 1942," the yeshiva man went on
broodingly. "At first Hitler had no long-range extermination
program, no 'Final Solution' staked out. Yes, he wanted to elimi-
nate Jews from Germany and the whole of Europe; but until the
war, the Nazis still had in mind the *forced* emigration of Jews
from Europe. Remember, Jenya?"

"I remember."

"The policy wasn't yet genocide. A couple of countries let
some refugees come in freely, over the border, without papers."

"I know."

"You know, I know, but the big powers, did they *want* to know, Jenya? I was in university at that time, studying science, languages—all so vital now, isn't it, Jenya?" he went on mockingly. "My family and neighbors were ready to leave, but who would have us? We were trapped not only in Poland, but also by something the Americans called 'quotas.' The old Psalmist liked to say, 'Plead my cause with them that strive against me,' and really, there were many people, important Jews, rabbis in America and England, pleading our cause, and some still are doing it. But the British White Paper of 1939 went against us, you remember. In fact, I was training for *aliyah* to Palestine, and I helped to organize my fellow students to prepare for *aliyah*. But the British were afraid, so they said, of antagonizing the Arabs, and stopped us with their bloody White Paper. And the crazy part of that is that the Arabs have gone with the Germans anyway! Then there were the Americans!"

"I've never spoken of it before," Jenya said, "but my father and mother dreamed of going to America. I have an uncle living in Newark, New Jersey."

"America, liberal America, has been worse than the British," Jacob went on dryly. "Sure they hate the Nazis, but no one who's pleading our cause can reach President Roosevelt's mind, or should I say heart? His own liberals in government, and the rabbis, have given him the evidence about the mass killings. Even his wife has been at him about it. But he's not doing anything, and he won't, Jenya. I can't imagine that he's anti-Semitic. But he's worrying about this war being called a 'Jewish war,' and he finds that politically dangerous. That's what our professors say he's worrying about—or rather what they *did* say. They're most of them dead now." Jacob's throat felt tight and dry, but he went on.

"You know, I can remember the Germans gleefully plastering all over their newspapers one White House press conference. This reporter had asked President Roosevelt, 'Would you recommend a relaxation of restrictions so Jewish refugees could come to America?' Wasn't that giving it to him straight?"

"And did he answer straight?"

"He did. He said, 'We have the quota system.' That's like saying, 'To hell with them,' because everyone knows that only a handful are allowed in under the quota system, and that practically excludes Poland with three million Jews. His Visa Division went further; they used the interesting excuse that refugees might be Nazi agents! So there you have it, Jenya—those pleading our cause are back to where they started."

"Are no refugees getting through, then?"

"A few. Now that America is in the war, there's a new slogan that the Allies are using—'Rescue Through Victory.' "

"And that's good, yes?"

"It *sounds* good. Of course, it forgets one thing. There may be very few Jews to rescue after victory."

They fell silent, Jacob studying the paper. He turned the pages, translating another decree, this one from the Gestapo, on how to be precise and efficient in executing the pattern of transfer of Jews from small towns to the bigger concentrations in city ghettos, complaining that Jews were playing "a prominent part in guerrilla attacks." Warning officials to register all Jews including infants.

"Oh, Rumkowski will comply, to the letter," Jacob said as he threw the paper down. "In Lodz he's the *balebos*—the dictator. He loves law and order as much as the Nazis, and I think he even believes that he's protecting his 'subjects.' He likes to call himself a real humanitarian, saving lives, and he parades his love for his Jewish 'subjects,' calling them '*my* workers,' '*my* Jews,' '*my* children.' He had protected *his* orphanage before the Germans came. And in the ghetto he'd give the kids sweets when he met them, and get them extra rations on holidays. So we began to believe him with the children.

"But still, no matter, everyone feared Rumkowski, because of his moods!" Jacob's voice was rasping and his eyes narrowed with anger. She put up a hand as though to stop the tirade, but Jacob began to pace the room and went on unheedingly. "No one knew what to expect from him from one moment to the next. He could console a person or he could consign him to the next transport. I remember last winter, for example, when we had to collect ice from the lake for the hospital, and there was no water that week, so no ice. Rumkowski came to the lake and asked a worker, 'Where is the ice?' And when the man said there was none, he struck the man with the heavy cane that he always carried and nearly killed him. The man was terrified of him, but what he feared most was that he'd be deported because there was no ice!

"The kids seemed to be something special, at least. Last Rosh Hashanah, the pupils and teachers of Lodz even presented him with an album of leather, signed by all of them, hundreds of them, thanking him for his kind protection, and they praised him as *Adonenu Ha-Nasi,* our lord, our prince. And the paradox is that the first ones he sent on the transport to be killed were *his* own orphans!"

Jacob's mood began to terrify Jenya.

"Please, Jacob, I think you should stop," she pleaded.

"He was a crazy man about this law-and-order thing. When the Nazis told him to register all children—'for work,' they said —we didn't want the children to register. It wouldn't be for work, and Rumkowski knew that, too. Very few kids turned up to register, and the parents began to hide them. That seemed to make him mad. So his Jewish Police and the Gestapo rounded up all the kids. They said don't worry, it was just that there was too much hunger and typhus spreading in the ghetto, and the children would be safer out of it. The really extraordinary thing is that Rumkowski, that lord, that prince, himself marched with the children to the railway station—you know, carrying out his orders 'completely . . . accurately.' "

Jacob turned back to Jenya, his eyes dark lakes of hatred in his pale face. "He said the Germans had spared *his* orphanage once so the people should trust him—nothing was going to happen to the children. The children trusted him. He led them, with their books and toys, and slices of bread and sweets which he'd distributed, to the transport, and the children got on. *All* the little ones up to age twelve."

"I don't want to hear any more!" Jenya cried.

"We never saw any of the children again."

Jenya trembled in the silence of the hut. For a moment she was back in the shambles of her flat in Korets, torn apart by the mindless death and destruction around her. She swayed and felt a scream rising inside her. Then she let Jacob's steely control cut into her growing emotion and held in the tears. He was the contemplative yeshiva scholar again, awed by the way history was overtaking humanity.

"Conspiracies, Jenya," he said. "All conspiracies."

"What do you mean?"

"Conspiracies—hatched in the dark recesses of man's mind. But they can be particularly revolting when they're hatched in the minds of 'liberals.' "

"Like this Rumkowski?"

"Like him . . . and some others."

"You know many Jewish Council leaders aren't like him," said Jenya with a shudder.

"Yes, I know."

"Our council president and the leaders in Korets were very brave. They wanted people to escape, go underground. They helped us."

"You were in a small ghetto."

"Very small. Well, it wasn't like Lodz or Warsaw."

"And you didn't have a Rumkowski." Jacob went to the wood stove, where a pot of coffee was bubbling, kept in readiness especially for partisans returning from missions. He poured himself a mugful, and brought a mug of the bitter black brew to Jenya. Well, now we've got our forest partisans, and underground partisans in the ghettos—in some ghettos—and the Rumkowskis be damned!"

"Many will die."

"The Talmud says it's better to know how to live, not how to die; and the partisans, given the chance, will take as many of the enemy as they can with them. The smell of the gas chambers stretches from Treblinka and Auschwitz and Maidanek to every ghetto in Europe today, if not to the politicians of all countries. So we have to find ways to survive, and the different ways we can fight back."

"In Warsaw?"

"Yes."

"In Lodz?"

"Most of those people can't. They're too brutalized."

"What *can* they do, then, Jacob?"

He turned away restlessly. "Nobody who has not been through it—I mean in a place like Lodz—can understand what's going on there."

"Is it so hopeless, then?"

"Nothing is hopeless, and a few of us got out. But by a fluke, because Rumkowski and his Jewish Police, never mind the Gestapo, are dead against any underground: they claim their policy saves Jews. In Warsaw and Vilna ghettos, it's different. They're trying to find ways to fight. Somehow."

He was pacing again, talking to himself, trying to reassure himself, then, seeing how his moods were affecting Jenya, he paused and said suddenly in a lighter tone, "Jenya, I'm sorry. But it's the first real talking I've done for a long time, and it just kept pouring out. Listen, let me tell you a *funny* tragic story. How can a gas chamber story be funny? you may ask. But it's true, because the Gestapo can be so damned efficient! I read it in an underground newspaper.

"There was this train filled with Jews being transported to Treblinka, and it came to a halt somewhere along the way. The wife of a German officer was waiting on the platform, and she thought it was a routine passenger train, so she got on with her two children. The Gestapo actually helped them to get on. She was so occupied with one thing and another and her children that it wasn't until she got to the camp that she realized her mistake. But at the destination, the Germans wouldn't accept her story—that she didn't belong on this train, that she was married to a German officer and so on—and anyway, she'd accidentally discovered their secret: that the Germans were taking Jews to be gassed and cremated. So she was taken with her children to the gas. How's that for efficiency?"

"I'm sorry for her children."

"Well, don't be," he said abruptly. "Think of the Lodz children, who got an official escort to *their* train."

Misha had arrived with Mottele and Lyonka. He was delighted to see Jacob on his feet, looking infinitely better, strong enough now to be useful. He also took in the tension in the little hut, but decided to ignore it.

"I'm glad to find you well again, Jacob."

"I feel fine, Diadia Misha. I want to thank you—"

"Thank Jenya," Misha interrupted crisply. "Now, I'm moving camp to a site near village Buda. My unit commanders and I have decided that we can help those villagers as well as ourselves. The Germans were very busy there until recently. They liquidated Buda's sawmill, and burned a lot of houses down, and drafted the young men into the army. The villagers understandably hate the Germans and want to help partisans. Village Buda will give us a stable base, and we can help them get rehabilitated, too."

Jacob's face fell. "I was thinking in terms of some mission," he began.

"This is a mission, and an important one for all of us," said Misha. "It's time we had a bit of civilized living again. We'll rebuild their school, and for a start I want you and some other teachers in it, and put our own kids into the school, too. Village Buda, incidentally, will give us a fine observation position."

"You're the commander," said Jacob, only barely concealing his disappointment. "But when may I brief you on conditions in Lodz ghetto?"

"Later, Jacob," Misha promised. "I want my commanders to hear it, too."

"All right."

"Now, then, Mottele, go with Jacob and Jenya to the family camp, and help the people to move."

Judge the poor and fatherless;
Do justice to the afflicted and destitute.
Rescue the poor and needy;
Deliver them out of the hand of the wicked.

P S A L M 82:3, 4

8

At the time that Diadia Misha moved his camp to the outskirts of village Buda, there were no fewer than twenty-five other major Jewish partisan units operating in the forests and swamplands of Eastern Poland, Lithuania, Byelorussia, the Ukraine, Yugoslavia. Ragged little partisan groups, with no military standing, no connections with the outside world, no news about the war, no liaison between their fighting units, yet they knew instinctively that if *they* had taken to the forests to resist and fight, others like them must be doing the same thing. But for the most part, the great Jewish centers of Warsaw, Lodz, Cracow, with their ghetto concentrations, were cut off from both forests and partisans, for only Jews living in villages near the open forest could hope to reach the partisans.

By summer of 1942, hundreds of thousands of Jews had perished, by gas, by starvation and disease, by degradation and forced labor. The world at war seemed to be duped, or uncomprehending, about the enormity of the crimes against the Jews; and curiously enough, many Jews themselves were duped by letters arriving in the ghettos from those previously transported and killed, for the letters said that they were working under good conditions, and the fabrications were accepted as bona fide in the ghettos as well as in many world capitals. The forest fighters were not duped. They accepted no hearsay and suspected everyone.

The Gentile partisan units took in only those who were strong, healthy and vengeful, who brought weapons with them, and some Jews managed to join them by hiding their identities. In contrast, Diadia Misha and most Jewish units took in *all* Jews because they were Jews. Jewish groups like Misha's emphasized three aspects in their fighting aims and fighting style: *revenge* —which had the highest priority; *survival*—not only for themselves but also for any poor and needy Jews who sought them out; *the price*—taking as many enemy lives with them as possible, should the Jews go down.

Diadia Misha never ceased to wonder how his fellow Jews, pacifists throughout history and by nature, could, without training, sophisticated weapons or psychological preparation for war, turn themselves practically overnight into warriors like the Maccabees of old! Whether or not they had a historic Covenant with God, the Jews of the forest certainly felt the covenant with one another.

But the Jewish partisans lacked the traditional requisites of organized warfare—coordinated headquarters; a central intelligence unit to get news to the outside world and bring in news from abroad; military hardware; lines of supply.

They had to depend on their own powers of improvisation; and on the good will of forest villagers (which was in short supply)—or take weapons, food and clothing by force. But *all* units didn't operate along compassionate lines like Misha's; the conditions were sometimes too dangerous for the smaller Jewish units. Rumor came that one small camp near ghetto Mir had refused to take in Jewish survivors, and had sent them away.

All through the region at the Polish-Russian border, where the dense forests could afford them protective retreats, Jewish partisan leaders and their units realized they were probably living on borrowed time, that they were few against the many. Misha had heard that partisan candidates for one detachment —the Atlasites, led by Dr. Yehezkel Atlas from a town near Lodz, who was called the "Little Doctor"—were asked the same blunt question: "What do you want?" And the answer *had* to be: "I want to die fighting!"

Of course, everyone hoped to live long enough at least to see the war turn.

Until then, the growing objective of Misha's unit and indeed of all Jewish partisans was first to group and establish themselves as *Jewish fighters* against the adversary; then to try to make contact with their partisan counterparts, and with the Soviet High Command in Moscow.

Village Buda, when Misha and his partisans reached it, was a barren little place, denuded by the Germans. Its fields were sandy and unsown; its industry, the sawmill, had been dismembered and shipped to Germany. Its young men had been drafted into the German Army. The peasants needed everything—food, farm animals, help in the fields to survive.

Misha fixed camp and a family site in the forest near Buda. He posted guards on trails leading to the village, and he went then into Buda with a detachment of partisans to set up an observation post. Buda was typical of all the forest villages. The peasants lived close together, in clusters of painted wooden huts, some decorated on top with carvings of birds, and with tiny double windows against the cold winters. The people came out of their houses and gave Misha and his men a cautious welcome. They did not know that these were Jewish partisans, nor did Misha enlighten them. All they saw were the ragged uniforms of no distinct army, the belts of cartridges and the rifles; and the villagers' tentative smiles were touched with fear.

Diadia Misha wanted to allay the fear at once.

"How about a concert to celebrate our arrival?" he asked his youngest partisan. "Maybe some of their own folk songs and some Russian stuff. What do you say, Mottele?"

"I say yes," said Mottele.

The village square with its cobbled lanes leading to a church, with its handsome pear trees and skinny pines, reminded Mottele of Ovruch again; except that this time he didn't have to line up with beggars, and there were no Germans to count. As he took out his violin and began to tune it, he saw the children come running; then their mothers and some old people started over. His fingers began to dance nimbly over the strings, and by the time he was into his first folk song, a good crowd had gathered and made a circle around him, their worn, tired faces creasing into smiles as they recognized the song. The children began to clap hands to the tune and the smallest ones to skip around like happy grasshoppers.

Mottele closed his eyes. He imagined, as he fiddled on, that his sister, Batya, was among the children, clapping her hands to the sweet notes. It was Friday night before the Sabbath, and Batya always asked him for a song before *Shabbes*. His mother was taking fresh-baked *challah* from the oven, and he and his sister could smell the aromas of the delicate, braided, cakelike bread, and of the *lokshan* soup and roast chicken ready for the *Shabbes* table. *Erev Shabbes*, Friday night, with the shining brass candlesticks in place on the polished dining room table, and near the candles the *Kiddush* cup, brimming with red wine. And Papa had come in from the mill, cleaned up and dressed up, wearing his *tallith* and skullcap. And then Mama, "bride of the week" for *Shabbes*, would call to Mottele to stop his fiddling and come along with Batya.

He would put the violin away and he and Batya would take their places at the table, but standing, while Mama—like all the Jewish mothers of the town at that hour—would light the candles and *bentsh licht*. Her arms would spread out above the flames, gesturing and drawing their light to her, as though drawing in the holiness of the night, murmuring the old prayer in Hebrew: "Blessed art Thou, O Lord our God, King of the Universe, Who hast hallowed us by His commandments and commanded us to kindle the Sabbath light."

The fantasy was so vivid that when Mottele finished the tune and opened his eyes, bowing to the warm applause, he was surprised to find he had been crying. Angrily he stared up at the late-afternoon sun, shading his eyes as though its glare had stung them, and he wiped his eyes and shouted to the crowd, "Now I have a special one!" He was dimly aware that Lyonka had seen his tears, and he was embarrassed.

"I hope it's not the *Horst Wessel*," an old woman called boldly.

"Not a chance," Mottele retorted. "Listen, we made this one up ourselves. It's called the 'Partisan March.' Lyonka, help me start it, will you?"

Lyonka grinned and nodded, and as Mottele played, Lyonka gave the peasants the words, which his father had composed:

Days of suffering and pain
Go ever onward,
And nights of fear and hope
Follow them.
The heart is full of horror,
Finding no rest.
Nevertheless, we want to live
And see the moment of vengeance!

It is not life nor even death,
To live always in fear and horror.
Isn't it better to die
A heroic death on the battlefield?

Young and old—come to the woods!
Run away from the ghetto!
Ten will die,
Ten will survive,
Forward . . . to battle!

Diadia Misha stood at the edge of the crowd, enjoying the moment, zestfully singing with his partisans. He saw Lyonka's arm go around Sarah as the music gathered momentum, but the girl drew away. Misha shrugged. Silly, rebellious girl, wasting time. This wasn't Korets. There would never be Korets again. No time for courting and the usual amenities. The only thing of value was mutual trust and mutual love. The only time they had was the present!

Mottele started another song. The children began to dance again, and as he quickened the tempo, the older people began to clap hands to the beat.

Misha saw Jenya, who was standing with Jacob. She, too, was clapping with gusto. She and Jacob stood close together, and when the music and clapping paused, Jacob took her hand and held it tight. Misha wished that Sarah could find some peace, too.

It was growing dark, and Misha and his men had a rendezvous with a house on a hill; he could see it from where he stood in the square. He'd realized that the house overlooked the main road leading to Narovna, the next town, and decided to make it their observation post. He now signaled to Lyonka to come.

"When Mottele's finished this one, bring him and Ivan over. We're going to pay a visit to our new observation post."

"Where's that, Papa?"

"Up on the hill. We're going to help them farm up there."

Ivan, the big former policeman from Ovruch, an obvious Gentile, was a good ally to bring along on the mission. The hill to the house was steep and stony; as they approached the top the men and the boy became aware that they were being watched from an open doorway. A very bent, beshawled old woman stood there, leaning on a cane, and to Mottele she looked like a witch, with her wizened face and thin, pointed nose and thin mouth. She must be about a hundred, the boy thought.

"How are you, Grandma," Misha said cheerfully. "We've come to talk to you. May we come in?"

"And can I stop you, with your guns?" she said in a cracked voice, affecting indifference. They entered a dimly lit room which held a wooden table and benches and a chest of drawers, and the uninvited guests sat down at the table. The old woman stood a distance away, eying them with hostility. Misha explained. The Germans were gone, but they could return, he said. This village was on a strategic road to the Russian front, so a group of his partisans, about ten, would be stationed near her house, which would be their observation post. The men would live in her cowshed and have their own field kitchen—"and you can use it, too, Grandma, if you like"—and they would help with the field work when not on patrol.

"They'd better stay out of my house," she threatened.

"None of my men will inconvenience you," Misha promised. "Now we've brought you a small present, Grandma."

He told Lyonka and Ivan to put the sacks they'd been carrying on the table. The contents brought a gasp and the first smile from Grandma. There were salt, some deer meat and bread inside.

"Now, those are presents!" she exclaimed. "The Germans took everything, and wanted mushrooms, but my little orphan was afraid to go in the forest for the mushrooms." She touched the sacks with shaking hands but she seemed to be afraid no longer. She put a little from each sack on the table, and told Lyonka where to hide the remainder of her presents in the wooden chest.

"I'll make you a pot of tea," she said. "Mirel! Come, come, child!" she called. "It's all right!"

In a moment, a little girl of about ten years ran into the room and threw herself against Grandma, burying her face in the other's shawl. She was barefoot but well washed, and wore a long cotton dress. She held Grandma tight and wouldn't look at the visitors.

"These are friends, Mirel, it's all right, these are partisans. Don't be afraid, child," Grandma said, and stroked Mirel's hair. The girl looked up slowly, and stared at the men and at Mottele with frightened eyes.

"Come on, Mirel, eat something," said Mottele.

But the girl shook her head, gave Grandma a kiss and ran from the room. Mottele watched her go with a thoughtful frown.

"Who was that?" he asked.

"Mirel's my little orphan."

"Your grandchild, then?"

The old woman didn't reply at once, but busied herself making the pot of tea which she then brought to the table. "I've lived alone here for thirty years. I'm a widow, and my only son died in the First World War. But the good Lord sent Mirel to me, a good girl, very kind, and she'll take care of me in my illness and old age."

"So she's *not* your grandchild?" asked Mottele.

"Well, I like to *think* she's mine. We take care of each other."

Misha and the others remained silent during the exchange, and now Mottele, on an impulse, cut two portions of the bread.

"I'll just take Mirel's out to her," he said politely. "She's probably shy with so many of us around. We'll eat ours outside."

"Want me to come with you?" asked Ivan.

"No."

"Go ahead, Mottele," said Misha. "Grandma and I can have
our talk meanwhile over this good tea."

After half an hour, Misha and the others, well satisfied with
their new friend, prepared to leave. They walked over to Mottele, who was sitting with the girl on a log, their heads close in
earnest discussion. Their talk ceased abruptly with the partisans' appearance, but not before Misha had heard Mottele say
as he got to his feet, "Don't worry, Mirel. If the old woman is
bad to you, Diadia Misha and I will take you with us."

Mirel dashed back to the house and stood next to Grandma,
waving goodbye.

"And what was *that* all about?" Misha asked the boy crossly
on the way back to the village.

"Uncle Misha, the girl is Jewish!"

"What!"

"She's from Narovna, the next town. I had a feeling about her
from the start. She was frightened of me until I spoke Yiddish
to her. She told me her parents were shot to death by the
Germans."

"Go on."

"I had that feeling about her in the house, then when the old
witch—"

"Grandma . . ."

"All right, when Grandma was so vague about her, my feelings got very strong. Mirel said Grandma likes her and treats
her well, but she's been forbidden to tell anyone that she's
Jewish. It's for her own protection, Grandma says."

"She seems to be in safe hands, at least for the time being. We
must keep her secret, Mottele."

"And take care of her after the war?"

"If we stay alive."

"I'd be interested to know," said Lyonka, "how she got to
Grandma."

"I asked her that. She said after her parents and all the older Jews were shot, the children of Narovna were collected and they expected to be killed, too. Most of them were, but a Ukrainian policeman came and picked out four kids who were healthy, and took them to his father's house. His father is a butcher, and he hid them because he wanted to sell them to the farmers he dealt with. Mirel said that Grandma bought her with a lamb and ten meters of cloth."

"Good God!" said Ivan.

They walked on in silence, broken by the crunch of their boots on the stony, ash-gray trail. Subconsciously, Lyonka was aware that there were no birds. Had the Germans shot them, too?

"And the other children?" he asked.

"When Grandma took Mirel, there were only two children left at the butcher's—Mirel's cousins, called Danya and Sonya."

"Maybe they're safely away, like Mirel?"

"Maybe. Maybe not."

Rescue me, and deliver me out of the hand
of strangers,
Whose mouth speaketh falsehood . . .

P S A L M 144:11

9

Now, in their new bivouac, the partisans found the occasional respite from military missions in welcome contrast to the earlier tempo. They had a field radio, zealously guarded by Popov, and on it news filtered in from time to time from underground radios. It helped morale immensely to be in touch with other camps.

The mortality rate of the partisan fighters had been depressingly high; it was high in the family camp, too, where a few infants, ill or undernourished before arriving at camp, had succumbed. Misha was determined to get some familiar routines moving. His people were too tired, too edgy, and because of their exhaustion were shooting badly.

Misha assigned a number of men to help the farmers sow their fields. And within the week, some partisans had rebuilt the one-room schoolhouse, and set up an easel for the blackboard. Children from the partisan camp now joined the village youngsters for lessons in arithmetic, writing and drawing, taught by Jacob and Ivan and a local woman.

Jacob created a *cheder* in a family camp hut, and for two hours each night the Jewish children huddled together and were drilled in Hebrew, sharing tattered prayer books that some old Jews had managed to bring with them, nibbling on bread and jam while Jacob told them folk tales from the Talmud. Mottele came to many of the classes, joining the little ones in the *cheder* text from the Torah, the five books of Moses, and in the ritualistic high singsong as they recited en masse. Many an old Jew sat against the wall, nodding and swaying to the familiar sounds, gratefully enfolded in the sounds of childhood and sweet learning.

And several times a week, Mottele called at Grandma's house. He became a favorite there, helping with chores, playing a tune or two on his violin until Mirel's bedtime.

But all the civilian activity, of course, remained secondary to military orders. There were days and nights when, without pause, Misha sent detachments to sabotage roads leading to the Russian front, or to ambush a troop train. In fact, such missions were beginning to be ordered and directed from Moscow itself. For Russia was at last in the process of organizing forest units into a Partisan Confederation which would eventually comprise brigades, battalions, platoons and details; and the High Command was emphasizing sabotage rather than attack strategy. Additionally, Moscow had opened schools for partisans, and graduates were being infiltrated to the front lines or dropped by parachute in the forest behind the front. Nor was Moscow unaware, it was clear to Misha, getting such data over the new field radio, of the dangerous anti-Semitism rampant not only among the German Nazis but also among many Ukrainian and Byelorussian forest units and villages. The Soviet's Highest Council of State sternly decreed:

"Because the enemy behaves in a beastly and barbaric manner, and practices total extermination of Soviet citizens of the Jewish nationality, it is hereby ordered to carry through their evacuation to the interior of Soviet Russia as a matter of priority."

The Jewish partisans remained skeptical.

It was in Buda during this period of relative ease that Lyonka and Mottele drew closer together. They found time to slip off alone, and go swimming and fishing in the streams nearby and once, showing off, Lyonka dispensed with his fishing pole and threw a grenade into the water. After it exploded, an enormous number of fish were tossed up—carp and whitefish and beluga. The two friends made a fire then, and had a fine feast before carrying the rest of the haul back to camp.

And Mottele showed the urban-bred Lyonka how to swim underwater for long periods: the boy broke off tall hollow reeds growing in the water, and putting the end of one in his mouth, he breathed through it, keeping the upper end above water while he swam below. One could watch the silently moving reed above, as the boy swam around completely unnoticed. Afterward they lay on the bank, staring up at the sky, enjoying their friendship.

Yet the agony was never far from either of them.

"Why did He let it happen?" Mottele asked one afternoon as they stretched out in the sun.

"What's that, Mottele?"

"I'd always been taught He was an all-powerful, all-merciful God, so why did He let it happen, then?"

"It's not the first time."

"That's an answer?"

"Some people think He has to keep on trying us, over and over again."

"Trying us? Like with old Job?"

"Something like that."

"Well, I don't go for that."

"All right."

"Do you?"

"It doesn't matter. The reasons, the rationale . . . even the rabbis can't get together on it, Mottele."

"What's their theory anyway?"

"I don't know. That it's not God, it's men. All men's doing."

"So where is God, to stop the men?"

"Oh, change the record, Mottele!"

"I'm sorry."

"It's just that—well, it's not important."

"Not important?"

"Living, going on living . . . and loving, that's important!"

"Loving?"

"Never to stop loving."

"You mean one another?"

"Well, little brother, I don't mean the Nazis!"

Mottele laughed then and stood up, staring at the carefree stream washing their feet, and his mood changed swiftly. "When are we going to attack Narovna, Lyonka?"

"What? Narovna? Why?"

"Grandma goes to Narovna every week, and she told Mirel that the butcher gets drunk and keeps threatening to kill the two children who are with him if he can't sell them. They're costing too much to feed, he says."

"*That's* what he told Grandma?"

"We have to rescue those children, Lyonka."

"Hey, hold on, boy! How do we know he still has them—today, I mean?"

"I can find out."

Lyonka rose on his elbow. "You in love with Mirel?" he joked. "Come on, little brother, you can tell me."

"Don't be stupid!" Mottele said angrily. "It's just that she reminds me of my sister, Batya, who'd be her age now—if she'd lived."

Lyonka looked rueful. "Sorry. Hell, we'll see what Papa says, Mottele."

But Diadia Misha was adamant. Narovna had a detachment of Ukrainian policemen and German soldiers, he said, and he had strict orders from the Moscow High Command not to attack it, but only to continue with sabotage missions for the present. Mottele fell silent under the reproof.

"Anyway," Misha went on, relenting, "how do we know the children are still there?"

"Grandma will tell us."

A few days later, Mottele went to Misha again. Grandma had been to village Narovna and had seen the children. They had looked thin and frightened.

"But they may be perfectly safe," said Misha.

"They're not," said Mottele stubbornly. "I feel sorry for them. Isn't there some way, Diadia Misha . . . ?"

"I'd like to save them, too, Mottele."

Misha called his unit commanders together and they weighed the pros and cons of a kidnapping. They decided that Mottele could have his way, try to get the children out, but according to their plan. Narovna was about to have a fair, and Mottele would essay his beggar act once again. From Grandma he knew that the butcher's house was near the Jewish cemetery, quite close to the forest, within which one or two partisans would be waiting. The details were mapped out: Mottele the barefoot beggar acting lost and forlorn, Ivan waiting in the forest to report in case anything went wrong, taking the machine gun with him just in case.

Then Sarah suddenly said *she* wanted to go with Mottele on this mission. She said she could act as a distraction, engaging the butcher or his wife, while the boy tried to get the children's attention and effect the rescue. Mottele was astonished. He knew the men were reluctant to send the girls on missions, using the excuse that they were indispensable for the wounded and for guard duties. But Sarah was determined.

"I *have* to go with Mottele," she cried out sharply. "I have my reasons!"

"Mottele is capable of scouting the area, and Ivan will be waiting. That's our plan," Misha said.

"I can be useful. Please! I'm going on this children's mission! It's important to me!"

"Let her go, Papa," Lyonka put in quietly. Sarah sent him a grateful look.

"Well, council?" asked Misha, obviously uneasy.

The men talked it over, and then unanimously agreed to amend the plan: Mottele the barefoot beggar would follow Sarah at a distance; and while Sarah engaged the butcher in some story about the sale of a cow that had broken its leg, the boy would try to get to the children.

The three partisans went along the wooded trail leading to village Narovna, the forest hushed and green. Mottele could have sung with happiness at the idea of going with Sarah on a mission. He admired her for standing up to the commander, and contrasted her demand that she should come with her bitter criticism of his going on other missions. And here they were, except for that great oaf Ivan, trailing behind both of them, really on their own, sharing Misha's trust in them, and their ability to improvise; well, to be precise, Sarah was leading at a distance of about thirty yards.

Mottele thought she looked beautiful. Her bare arms were swinging, her hair was tucked under a red kerchief, her loose peasant dress fell just below her knees. She turned around now and then to flash him a smile. He felt he was desperately in love with her, loving her even more than he did Lyonka or Misha!

The sunshine was bouncing off tree trunks, skittering over the trail, and the boy hummed the partisans' march as he held his distance. He was grateful that Lyonka had supported her decision, and wondered why Sarah sometimes seemed to be afraid of Lyonka.

They found their way, without any problems, to the butcher's shop. Mottele watched until he saw Sarah take her place at the end of a long queue, waiting her turn with the butcher, to bargain about her "cow." Then Mottele walked slowly to the back of the house and stared, without apparent interest, over a low fence at two children at work among the chickens and the woodpile. The little girl, about Mirel's age, was washing some laundry in a tub; the boy was gathering logs. Mottele looked all around him and saw they were alone, and he took a chance. He called over, "Danya, come to the fence!"

The boy looked at Mottele with fright, then at the girl, and the girl shook her head with vehemence, warning him to take no notice. And at first the boy went on with his work, but he was curious and edged to the fence.

"Your cousin Mirel asked me to give you regards," Mottele said, deliberately speaking in Yiddish.

"Where is Mirel? Who are you?"

"Listen, I'm Jewish, too, I'm a partisan, and Mirel is with us. And your father's with us, too, in our family camp in the forest. He wants you to come!"

The boy drew back, confused and big-eyed.

"You're lying! My father was killed!"

"I'm not lying!"

"Go away. I'm afraid."

"Listen, is this a lie? Your father's name is Josef, and he sent me to rescue you and the girl."

The boy was shaking with excitement and hope. This partisan, if that's what he was, certainly had the names of his family, he spoke Yiddish, he knew Mirel, and anyway, Danya was afraid of the butcher and his wife. The butcher beat him and Sonya when he was drunk, and threatened them with his knife. He ran back to the girl, and Mottele watched them having a whispered argument, then Danya half dragged the girl to the fence.

"You speak Yiddish, but so do a lot of Ukrainian people," the little girl whimpered. She looked strangely old, with watery brown eyes and uncombed hair, her long shapeless dress hanging on her like a sack. "Go away. If the butcher catches us talking to you, he'll kill us with his big knife!"

"No, let's go with him!" Danya cried.

"I'm afraid!"

"I'm going to go!"

"If Danya leaves and you stay," said Mottele, "the butcher will take it out on you."

"Hey, you two!" A woman's voice called, shrill and commanding, from inside the house. "I've got your soup. Hurry up!"

The children looked fearfully toward the house, then looked at Mottele, and the girl nodded.

"We're coming!" Danya yelled back, before they jumped over the fence and walked quickly away with Mottele.

At about the same time, Sarah had arrived at the head of the queue. She faced a large, florid, bald-headed man with hairy moles on his face. His once-white butcher's apron was smeared with bloody handprints. Sarah gave him her warmest smile.

"What'll it be, miss? My dinner's waiting."

"It's about my cow, sir. She broke her leg, and she'll have to be killed, and I was told to see if you want to buy her."

The butcher asked Sarah to come into the living quarters behind the shop. He could be interested, he said, but wanted to discuss the price. They entered a large and lavish room which was in remarkable contrast with his cluttered butcher shop: expensive carpets on the floor; heavy, ornate furniture; landscape paintings in gilt-edged frames hanging on the walls next to the usual holy pictures; a handsome sideboard, highly polished and adorned with a pair of tall silver candelabra. She was fascinated by the candelabra. She wondered from how many Jewish homes the policeman son had stolen the rich adornments.

Before the butcher could begin negotiating, his wife burst into the room, shouting, "The Jews have gone!"

"Rubbish!" said the butcher.

"It's true! They didn't come in for their meal, and I've looked everywhere for them!"

"Well, they won't get far! Listen, I took it on myself to raise two Jewish children, and all I get is trouble," he complained to Sarah, as though in self-protection for keeping Jews. "Now I've had enough. When I find them, I'll hand them to my son, who's a policeman. He can do what he likes with them. Wait here. I'll be right back and we can finish the deal."

He rushed out.

"You have your dinner," Sarah told the wife, "and I'll wait for your husband outside. All right?" She was anxious to be off, realizing that Mottele had accomplished his mission.

When she got outside she waited a moment, then walked rapidly toward the forest, where Ivan and Mottele would be waiting. The candlesticks on the sideboard haunted her. They were so like her mother's.

Mottele led the way back to camp, the children keeping joyful step beside him. He was silent as the boy chattered on about the coming reunion with his father. Finally Mottele told him, "I lied to you."

The children stopped, and Danya grabbed Mottele's arm.

"What are you saying? Where are you taking us?"

"Don't be afraid," Mottele said. "I had to lie."

"What about?"

"Your father isn't with us. Mirel and I decided I had to lie to convince you to come with me, and she gave me your father's name. It was the only way to make you leave that place!"

The boy began to cry, and the girl clung to him in terror and joined in.

"You lied!"

"I told you, I had to do it that way."

"My father's dead. Everybody's dead."

"No, Mirel's all right. You'll see."

"You're lying again."

"No, no, just wait. You'll see!"

Sarah took from her pocket a small paper bag and gave the children some bread and sweets. Then she took their hands and soothed them and kissed the little girl.

"Don't worry so. The partisans love children. You'll be safe with us," she said in Yiddish. "I love children."

Starting that night, Misha doubled the guard along the trail leading from Buda to Narovna. Eventually, he thought, the butcher would remember the Jewish child he had sold to Grandma, and Grandma's subsequent visits to Narovna; he and his son would speculate that partisans in Grandma's village had kidnapped the two children. Misha decided it was no time to take chances.

Grandma was none too happy, though, with Misha's order to house all three Jewish children in the family camp. She loved Mirel and was fiercely protective of the child, proud that for so long they'd kept their secret from the other villagers. But now she realized, with not a little shock, that Misha and most of his partisans were Jews, and she agreed that the children should stay together in the camp.

Misha told Grandma Mirel would come to help with chores on some days; and Sarah and Mottele would come on other days. Grandma agreed somewhat reluctantly. "And now, you be sure and control that child," she admonished, leaning almost double over her cane to hide her emotion. "I don't want her running alone in the forest."

"We'll be strict, Grandma," Misha said.

"And see that you feed her!"

"You're a good grandma—a good *bobeh*," Misha said, hugging her. And Grandma allowed a wisp of a smile to soften the moment before he left. The old lady understood only too well the sensitivity of the partisans about their most treasured human resource—children.

In any case, with all the moving around, the enemy not far from their doorstep, the sudden pulling up of camp, Jewish children were certainly safer among Jews. Jacob the yeshiva scholar, receiving the new little recruits into his *cheder*, summed it up in his blindingly realistic way: "God may have to square Himself with us one day," he told Jenya, "but at least *we* won't have to square ourselves with Him when it comes to the children."

It is darkness, and not light. . . .
Shall not the day of the Lord be darkness,
and not light?
Even very dark, and no brightness in it?

10

All too often now, the partisans felt their isolation; so many days and weeks in their limited war arena seemed to be of "darkness, and not light." Just how *was* the war going in the outside world? Who was for them, who against them? It was hard to assess, though they made occasional contact now, by their field radio, with other partisan units in the general area and one day a new recruit brought a leaflet with him, one of thousands being dropped by Soviet planes in the villages. Before an eager crowd of partisans, Jacob translated the leaflet from the Russian into Yiddish:

"The Soviet Union is proud of the forest fighters. The Russian factories are stepping up production of tanks and airplanes. But education and culture aren't being neglected. In fact, children of Russian soldiers are being educated in special schools while their fathers are at the front, and preparations are being made in England for a second front!"

A roar of excitement greeted the news, and a burst of handclapping. The children, while not understanding, clapped enthusiastically, so happy did everyone suddenly appear, especially the old ones. Jacob went on reading and translating, trying to contain his own emotion. "And workers in America and Canada are doing overtime in their factories to provide the most modern implements of war. Thousands of their soldiers are already in England, apparently in preparation for that second front! And it winds up with this appeal to us—look, to the partisans!"

Jacob held the leaflet up and pointed to the bold-faced, one-word headline: PARTISANS! He read: " 'Men and women fighting heroically in the forests against the despicable Nazis and Fascists, you are not forgotten! Do not slacken your glorious efforts! Carry on the sabotage! Derail the German trains! Whoever beats and kills your brothers is your enemy! The High Command of Partisan Units is continuing to expand!' "

After this, Misha's partisans intensified their sabotage missions; and the new efforts, which were surely being duplicated by other partisan units, unified them like passports of power. Misha began to withdraw men from the field work and sent them daily on the ordered missions. Mottele had been given the task of taking horses to pasture not far from camp, and sometimes he took Danya with him, for a horseback ride, or to banquet with him on the lush raspberry bushes.

Young Danya had quickly adjusted to life in the family camp, reveling in his new freedom, practically adopting Mottele, whom he imitated in everything. One day, after they had tied their horses to a tree and eaten their fill of the sweet raspberries, they stretched out together in lazy serenity, staring up at the bright midday sun. Mottele was on the verge of telling Danya they should start back when there was a noise of heavy footsteps on dried twigs. Mottele grabbed the younger boy and they threw themselves behind a bush. With terrified eyes, they watched two German soldiers coming down the trail, with automatic guns drawn. The soldiers trod slowly, looking around them as they came on, the first carrying a field phone and wires on his shoulder.

They passed within inches of the hidden boys and went on, until they came to a halt at a thickly branched oak. The first soldier handed the wires to his partner, then climbed the tree with his field phone. The partner now gestured to the soldier settled far up in the tree, then he began to walk back, trailing the telephone wire as he moved, shoving the wire into the ground and smoothing soil over it with his boot. Then he disappeared into the forest with the rest of the wire. It was all done in minutes, ending suddenly like a vanishing act.

Danya in his terror had been ready to run, but Mottele had kept the boy's head down and had restrained him. He waited until the receding footsteps were gone and the woods quiet again. Then he whispered, "That soldier in the tree is called a 'cuckoo.' He's a watcher for the Germans, and he'll stay up there with his telephone. He can report on everyone moving in the forest, and he can even direct the artillery later. The enemy uses 'cuckoos' whenever they're planning a big offensive, Danya, and we have to let Misha know."

"Then let's go, Mottele!"

"We will—soon."

"Now! Please!"

"First I have a job to do. Come on, Danya, be quiet and watch!"

Mottele led the way, crawling on his stomach behind the bushes, in the direction of the buried telephone wire. He took a long, firm twig and dug up a portion of the wire and pulled it to him; then, with his pocketknife, he cut the wire. He carefully reburied both ends, while Danya watched with admiration. Mottele wasn't sure of his actions; in fact, he was inwardly as terrified as the younger boy, realizing that someone would soon come about the cut wire; but he held his fear in, and they crept on toward the horses. Mottele untied them and led them quietly back along the trail, then he gave the signal to mount and the boys galloped hard back to camp.

Mottele was unprepared for his commander's reaction to his report on the dangerous adventure. Misha looked at him with such open commendation that the boy blushed. Misha delighted so in this boy and his shrewd instincts that he really wanted to embrace the lad, but he knew Mottele would resent that, especially in the presence of the others, so Diadia Misha shoved his hands inside his belt and said crisply, "This is important information, Mottele. We knew the Germans were concentrating a force in the villages near here, but you tell us that their troops are right on our doorstep! Mottele, can you go back there with several men and show them where that 'cuckoo' is hiding?"

"I can, Uncle Misha."

"I want him wiped out. Ivan!"

"Yes, Commandant!"

"You will be in charge, but be very careful. The Germans may already have checked the phone and found it doesn't work, and realize they've been spotted. They may bring up reinforcements."

"I understand, Commandant."

"Mottele will show you the way. Take seven or eight men with you. Meantime, until we wipe that gang out, I'll evacuate our sick and wounded to a safer place. Get going, Ivan."

"*Shalom*, Commandant," said Ivan, very pleased and solemn, as delighted as Misha with the boy.

Even before Mottele and the group reached the area where the "cuckoo" was hiding, the partisans knew that the enemy had discovered the wires had been tampered with. They were met with a rain of bullets. Ivan ordered Mottele to stay behind while they fought it out. The boy hesitated—he was carrying his gun—but he followed orders and climbed partway up a densely branched tree, from which he watched the action. The partisans were drastically outnumbered. Ivan shouted the order to retreat.

Mottele, watching the uneven battle from his perch, saw Ivan bring up the rear of his unit, then run for Mottele's tree. He had almost reached it, when he was shot. Ivan fell heavily. He tried to stand, but his right arm and left leg were shattered. He fell again and lay as though dead. Some Germans ran to the big Russian, while others kept up their fire on partisans as they retreated to the woods. From the direction of camp, Mottele could hear explosions and artillery fire.

Are the Germans attacking the camp, or are they only stepping on our mines? the boy wondered. He sat stiff with fear behind the branches, almost directly above Ivan and the Germans hovering over him. Uncertain about his next move, Mottele peered down miserably at the immobilized Russian. He was fond of the big, clumsy, protective fellow, especially since

Ivan had gone with him and Sarah to rescue the children. Now his huge frame lay prostrate and vulnerable among dead leaves and Germans, and Mottele fumed against his own helplessness.

He watched several Germans leave, to carry their own wounded into the forest, but two remained with guns drawn, and suddenly Mottele heard Ivan moan, and saw him move his good arm on the leaves. One of the soldiers shouted something, then the two Germans bent over his friend and tied his hands and feet with leather straps. The boy shivered, knowing what that meant—they would take Ivan away, and he would be tortured first, to get information, then killed. Mottele steeled himself for what he knew he must do.

He pointed his pistol down at the Germans and fired a shot at each of them. The soldiers let out screams, and both went down. Mottele withdrew into the branches. The sound of the shots brought a few German comrades racing back to the tree; one soldier lay dead, the other, shot in the throat, was writhing in agony. The Germans stared about in vain for the source of the shots; then apparently decided to come back later for their dead comrade and Ivan, for now they carried off only the wounded soldier, and disappeared with him into the woods. The whole episode had taken just a few minutes, but until their footsteps were gone, Mottele wondered if his own end had come.

Now the woods lay in eerie silence and no living thing stirred. Even the leaves were motionless. Mottele remained quite still, straining to detect some sound that would signal the enemy's return. He knew the partisans would come looking for him and Ivan; it was tradition to bring back their dead when they could, and bury them with military honors. The Germans knew this, too, and could be returning for that reason. And Mottele wasn't sure that the partisans had wiped out the "cuckoo," who he feared might still be on his telephone perch not far away. Mottele shivered with indecision, but all did seem serene, and he had to take a chance. He looked in the direction of the "cuckoo." Silence. Mottele slid down and hurried to untie Ivan's hands and feet. Then he shook the big fellow.

"Come on, Ivan, you have to get up!"

Ivan opened his eyes, then closed them.

"We've got to hurry. The Germans will be back!"

On the word "Germans," Ivan opened his eyes again and tried to smile as he recognized Mottele.

"Water," he whispered.

Mottele saw a field flask hanging on the belt of the dead German. It was no time to think of feelings; he tore the flask off the man he had just killed, and got the stopper off. The flask held not water but, mercifully, brandy. Mottele forced some into Ivan's mouth. By struggling hard, he got Ivan to his feet, but the big man sagged and began to sink down.

"Save yourself, Mottele," Ivan whispered.

"No fear! You wouldn't leave me behind, would you? Come on!"

"I can't walk."

"You'll walk!"

"Can't do it, lad."

"Lean on me, Ivan!"

Mottele forced more brandy into him. Then Ivan drew himself up and leaned on the boy, mumbling, "I'll never forget this."

"Let's move. Lyonka and the others will be looking for us!"

They stumbled into the bushes. There Mottele took a moment to tear away Ivan's trouser leg, and he washed the wound with brandy, the way Sarah had told him that partisans cared for wounded in the field. Next he tore off his shirt and bandaged Ivan's leg and arm to try to stop the bleeding. With the big man leaning heavily on him, Mottele moved him slowly from bush to bush, from tree to tree, in the direction of camp.

It was all painfully slow, measured, Mottele was to recall later, by inches and groans and bandages coming loose. Then Mottele heard the first joyful signal—Lyonka's birdlike whistles, two short and one long—and knew that the partisans were near. He sat the big man down and put two fingers in his mouth to reply in kind. The two friends continued the whistling, running in each other's direction, following the sounds. Mottele sprang into Lyonka's arms, and they held each other.

"Come quickly, Lyonka, Ivan is wounded. He's not far." And Mottele led the way back to Ivan.

One dark episode at least was over. Ivan reported that he was sure he'd got the "cuckoo" with a grenade before being shot. But camp itself was a shambles: the partisans had fought all the way back into camp, and the Germans had operated with mortars and heavy machine guns. The enemy had been winning, until a partisan unit of fifty men got to the Germans from their rear and drove them off. The partisans had four dead and seven wounded. Misha said they must shift camp again.

But first it was important to get to village Buda, because, Misha went on, trying not to sound worried, Sarah had gone there earlier in the day to help Grandma, and she hadn't returned. He sent Lyonka and Mottele and three others to reconnoiter.

This had been one of the longest days in Mottele's life, but he had pleaded with Misha to be allowed to go, and said he wasn't tired, and that he had to be with Sarah; so Misha gave the lad into Lyonka's care and the two friends rode together to Buda.

The village seemed deserted. The Germans had not attacked, they noted to their relief, or so it seemed in the twilight of the dying day. Chickens swaggered about in the small enclosures; a cow with heavy teats waited patiently in the miller's yard, looking around and lashing her tail. On the surface the place seemed to be untouched, but when a small boy, dressed only in his torn shirt, wandered out of a hut, his mother ran after him and rushed him back indoors. There were no people in the square, where normally the villagers liked to meet or promenade. Mottele and Lyonka left their horses and walked the hill to Grandma's house. No one was inside.

They found Grandma lying in the backyard, in a pool of blood.

Lyonka cradled her in his arms.

"I want a priest, I want to confess," she whispered.

"Dear Grandma, dear *Bobeh,*" Mottele said, and he wept and held her hand. "Dear *Bobeh,* what happened?"

"I need a priest."

"Where's Sarah?" Lyonka murmured.

"The partisans went to defend the villagers," she whispered, forcing the words out. "Then the butcher and his son came up here, and they were looking . . . you know? Sarah saw them coming, and she was taking me out the back way so we could hide, when they came. I'm dying, Mottele. I must confess."

"You're a good Grandma, don't worry," Lyonka said, cradling her closely, stroking her hair. *"Bobeh,* tell me, where's Sarah?"

"The butcher said, 'That's the girl who came into my shop when the Jews escaped. That's the girl.' They hit her, and took her behind the hill."

"Oh, my God, goddamn you, God," Mottele moaned.

Lyonka carried Grandma into the house. He put her on the bed and covered her with a blanket. Mottele tried to give her some water, but she shook her head.

"Go and look for Sarah," she whispered.

"We'll come back with a priest, *Bobeh,"* said Mottele.

He took her hand, and kissed her cheek, but the hand grew cold in his and he let it slip to the blanket, staring at Grandma in horror.

A great sob came from Lyonka, and then he closed Grandma's eyes.

They left the house and went behind the hill. They found a trail, freshly marked by someone's being pulled or dragged. They carried their automatics in their hands as they dashed from tree to tree, watching for any Germans or Ukrainians still around. The woods had grown dark, and they cast no shadows as they ran. They did not have far to go.

Sarah lay where the two men had left her. Her clothes and shoes had been torn off and were scattered near her hair. She lay between two trees in some sour-smelling mud. She was smeared with the mud as though someone had attempted to camouflage her inert, vulnerable shape. Her head was bloodied where it must have hit the ground. There was blood on her still spread legs. One arm lay over her eyes, and the other hand dug deeply into the mud.

Lyonka covered her with his jacket. He lifted her in his arms.

He concentrated on holding the girl carefully, restraining his terrible grief.

"Is Sarah dead, Lyonka?"

"No, she's not dead."

"You sure?"

"I'm sure, thank God!"

Mottele spat violently. "Why thank Him?"

The boy gathered up her clothes and shoes.

"She going to be all right, Lyonka?"

"Yes. It's just that . . . she was afraid of the dark."

"What?"

"She was afraid it would get dark again."

"Sarah wasn't afraid of anything!"

"Just the dark."

Mottele led the way back. He prayed. He hated God with all his heart, but he prayed hard. He was crying, and he didn't know what else to do with his feelings. He cursed God and he prayed, and demanded: Sarah must live, she must go on living!

"You can do that!" he demanded as he prayed.

He gripped the automatic, which had already killed that day. He led the way to the horses, looking around as they went to make certain they were quite alone.

Hast thou found me, O mine enemy?

11

The partisans stood in military formation, yarmulkes on their heads, saying Kaddish for their dead. Then, in a clearing away from the trail, they buried seven young men in a mass grave, spaded the soft earth over them, and camouflaged the area with branches.

Diadia Misha waited several days before giving the command for two separate actions. The first action was to prepare to pull up camp and move north. He knew that the village Buda was no longer safe, should the partisans remain. The peasants were distressed to lose them, for Misha's men had been good to them, helping to rehabilitate the plundered village, rebuild the school, work in the fields, even bring a measure of music into their lives; but both sides agreed that their beneficial relationship had been destroyed.

Misha had decided to join forces with another partisan unit some kilometers northward in the Ukraine. He worried privately over the move, for the northern unit was mostly Gentile. They would have to risk their reception, Misha argued with himself, and anyway, the Partisan High Command encouraged such mergers to unify strategy.

The second action needed little discussion: to revenge themselves on the butcher and his family.

"Since you know that terrain, Mottele, you will go with Lyonka," said Misha. "You are to throw grenades from the cemetery onto the house, blow the place up, and withdraw. I don't want the whole bloody garrison aroused before you leave. Be accurate and be careful."

The tragedy of Grandma's murder and Sarah's rape had filled
the camp with an overwhelming rage, and several partisans had
been ready to take the mission on without waiting for instructions; but the commander knew that the two friends would
want to handle this one. Lyonka and Mottele were to rendezvous later with the rest of Misha's unit at the new site.

It was getting dangerously light by the time Mottele and
Lyonka reached Narovna. They had been riding in silence, and
the forest, bathed in early-morning mist, was eerily still as the
village came into view. They left their horses then and went on
foot into no-man's-land. It struck Mottele that despite his exhaustion, every nerve in his body seemed sharply alert. He did
not want to die, and he did not want Lyonka to die, but he and
Lyonka knew that the animals who had committed such out-
rages must be dealt with, destroyed.

He stepped on some dry twigs, and the noise carried in the
forest stillness.

"Be quiet!" Lyonka whispered.

"I'm sorry."

Creeping from the woods into the cemetery, they got unnoticed to a point within grenade distance from the butcher's
house. It, too, was cloaked in the dim morning light, but Mottele
could make out a woman's figure—the butcher's wife—in the
yard, feeding the chickens. Lyonka gave the signal, and they
threw their grenades simultaneously.

The first two bombs hit the yard from which Mottele had
rescued the children. A moment later, two more were lobbed
onto the house. The explosions shook the ground and blew up
the chickens, and the house itself now went up in fire. The
smoke curled toward the cemetery. Mottele and Lyonka were
already running back to the woods, but not before they heard
the butcher's dying wife scream, "My husband, my son . . . !"

The two partisans got back to their horses, and without a
word they started off in the direction of their rendezvous with
Misha. Nazi patrols might soon be after them, but the patrols
would be reluctant to venture too deeply into partisan territory.
Lyonka counted on that as he began to race his horse madly
forward, Mottele keeping up as madly.

"Let *them* do the confessing now, Grandma!" Mottele
shouted into the wind.

By late morning, Misha and his detachment arrived at their
destination, in the northeastern Zhitomir forest, the campsite
of the Saborov brigade. His tired and ragged little army, a
strange mix of soldiers and ancients, seemed to move in al-
mighty silence, the mothers carrying babies and bread in their
shawls, the stumbling old people holding on firmly to toddlers.
Some of the sick and wounded were on litters. And all were
apprehensive about their reception, especially Diadia Misha. So
he was unprepared for the warm and enthusiastic greeting
from the Saborov squadron leaders, who grabbed the partisans
and shook their hands and hugged them, and brought out
chocolate bars for the children.

Why, we're being hailed like conquering heroes, Misha
thought with awe. What could be the meaning?

"Uncle Misha reporting—" he began to no one in particular.

"Don't we know that, you old Cossack!"

"We already got it over the radio!"

"The Partisan High Command told us to expect you!"

"Old man"—this to a bearded ancient—"you look like the
bishop of Zhitomir!"

"Uncle Misha, I have something to tell you." Misha found
himself being addressed by a young commander, who was es-
corting him to headquarters. What this tough courteous young
partisan—he seemed hardly more than a boy—had to say was
that there must be just one command. "Our commandant was
killed last week," he said. "It has been agreed among us . . . I
mean I have the honor to invite you to take command of our
joint forces."

Misha's eyes misted. The boy held himself with such dignity,
such style.

"I have the honor to accept," he said gravely.

They shook hands.

"The news is getting better, Diadia Misha. Come; our radio-
man will give you the latest."

On their way to the communications hut, Misha saw to his

relief that this large encampment seemed like a forest village, built for permanency. Aboveground were dozens of rude but sturdy shelters; metal doors stood open to underground bunkers already built for the bitter, snowbound winters. In a fenced-in corral were numerous horses, goats, cattle. Only a family camp would be needed for his civilians.

Several of his men were waiting in the communications hut.

"Dr. Atlas, the 'Little Doctor,' is the big news," the radio officer said. "His Atlasites are operating in the Bialystok district to the north of us. They just made a surprise attack on a German-Lithuanian garrison, and killed about fifty on the very place where the Derechchin Jews were murdered."

"I thought the Germans had killed all the Derechchin Jews."

"No; Dr. Atlas had some survivors in his unit."

"That 'Little Doctor,' " marveled Misha. "He's astonishing! You know what he tells his men? 'You're only getting a reprieve from death,' he tells them, 'so you've just time to avenge yourself on the enemy.' "

"That's the best propaganda!"

"Propaganda? Truth!"

"The 'Little Doctor' is just a realist!"

"Naturally. Or would you expect his men to tell the bastards: Don't fire on us or we'll fire on you!" someone mocked.

"So go on, kibitz, but Atlas is right!"

"Of course, but don't we know we're all living on borrowed time?"

"Dr. Yehezkel Atlas is a realist *and* a medical man," Misha put in evenly. "And that means he has no illusions about life and death. He merely wants to remind everyone that we're in this thing together—to the end."

"No choice," persisted the joker.

"Wrong again," retorted Misha. "We made our choice, didn't we?"

Over the next few weeks, Misha's partisans settled down on the new site, which was, gratifyingly, far better equipped than the old. They built the family camp for the civilians, and a hut there for Jacob's *cheder*. Simultaneously, Misha intensified the sabotage missions, especially against supply convoys. Misha could perceive no distinctions luckily, between Gentile and Jewish partisans—they fought as one, motivated by their personally felt convictions: smugglers alongside Hasids, peasants with former tailors and engineers. He sent his missions out mostly at dusk—the best time for sabotage and raids. So disciplined by now were the partisans that the majority returned safely. Every night the communications hut was the focus for word about other partisan detachments.

The news was dominated by the "Little Doctor" and his Atlasites.

They had attacked village Ruda in the Zhitomir and driven out German troops, but they had had to give it up soon after, "not before we were able to reequip ourselves, however, with arms and supplies for the coming winter," they reported.

"The *health and welfare* of the partisans and the family groups," Dr. Atlas himself radioed, "must have priority. Therefore, we're storing food and medical supplies underground and I recommend the same to our comrades for this coming winter of 1942. Long live all the resisters!"

The bulletins from the Atlasites were the best part of the news, but suddenly they became fewer. Dr. Atlas and his men were meeting "tougher resistance from Hitler's troops." Nazi commanders were apparently withdrawing soldiers from the Eastern front, they radioed, to try to put an end to the forest "bandits" and their derailments of troop trains. The few bulletins remained optimistic nevertheless: "We have burned the bridges over the Niemen. . . . Today we derailed a train near Reshanka Station. . . . We have brought down a German aircraft. . . . We're attacking the German garrison near Novogrudok. . . ."

Jacob was assigned to write the bulletins in Yiddish, Mottele to copy them in Ukrainian, and so the camp dwellers got their first "newspaper." Demonstrating such contact with other major partisan units continued to be the best morale builder, and soon Jacob was adding bits of international news: London and

the British seacoast were being blitzed, but now the Allies were
bombarding Rome. . . . The American army was marching on
Tunis. . . . A South African army had attacked the Germans from
the south. . . . The Germans still occupied Byelorussia, and they
had Leningrad under siege, but the Russians were hitting back
hard in the Stalingrad-Rostov region. . . .

The little paper cheered everyone up. The people waited for
the war to turn. There were even rumors that it would soon be
over . . . but when? Communications often broke down, and
when that happened, the blackout on news became agonizing.

Then one morning, when Jacob and Mottele were in the
communications hut, a bulletin flashed in from the Atlasites. It
was explicit and shattering:

"Dr. Atlas, hero of Lodz and Slonim and Derechchin, was
fatally wounded while leading an attack on German troops near
Wielki Oblovic. He told us— these were his last words—'Lads,
pay no attention to me. Go on fighting!' We Atlasites are continuing his battle. Shalom, comrades!"

The silence in the little hut was enormous and oppressive. It
was war, and death was their constant companion; but the "Little Doctor," whom none knew personally, had been a heroic
father figure to them. Jacob's pen, which had been writing
steadily, had stopped and he gripped it like a gun.

"Nityatamnu—we have been orphaned again," he said quietly.

That afternoon, Jacob went with Jenya and Mottele to the
hospital hut where Sarah still lay.

Her physical wounds had healed, but her will to face reality
again seemed suspended. She wouldn't eat, drank only water,
and talked to no one. She had drawn a curtain of silence around
her, and lay now so still as to appear to be waiting for death.

Lyonka and Mottele had tried in vain to talk her out of her
trancelike state. Lyonka had used soft words, then angry words,
accusing her of pampering herself, trying to provoke her into
some response, but she only stared at him as though understanding his motive and rejecting it. She was dead to all appeals.
Only once did she react, when Mottele read her Dr. Atlas's

admonition to store the medical supplies, and that was with a shrug, as if to say, "Why bother?"

Diadia Misha came and told her, trying to sound tough, "All right, Sarah, so you were raped. That saying it loud enough? Now you listen to me: we've all of us been raped. We know what it is to be raped by animals and we're not dying of shame. I need your help with our larger membership here. There are many people wounded and ill, and not enough medical supplies or medical workers. Think that over, Sarah, but don't take long. I can't spare you."

Mottele came again and again. He sat on the edge of her cot, and held her hand and kissed it and told her, "I used my gun, Sarah, and I'm glad I had it to use," doing his best, like Lyonka, to provoke her. But she turned away from him, too, trying to escape.

"Sarah, don't be ill anymore, please!" Mottele pleaded. She lay in stubborn silence.

Now it was Jacob's and Jenya's turn.

"Listen, Sarah, the war's changing," Jenya began. "We're winning; it came over the radio. The partisans are operating inside Paris, even in broad daylight. We had a bulletin that women in the Paris partisans are fighting Nazis in the streets!"

Still the silence, freezing Jenya out.

"You won't shut me out—I won't have it, Sarah!" Jenya suddenly stormed. "I can't do all that work with the wounded men. I don't know what to do without you! I'll—I'll take you and shake you, the way you shook me once!"

"Come on, Jenya," said Jacob.

He started to take Jenya's hand and lead her away, then changed his mind. The death of the "Little Doctor" still overwhelmed and embittered Jacob, and he hated the feel of death around him. This was no time for self-pity.

"Don't be stupid, Sarah," he said in a brutal tone. "You can will yourself to die; that's easy. Or you can live. The Talmud says it's better to know how to live than how to die. We've got a word for it—*ueberleben*—to endure, to survive, to live, no matter what, through all of this!"

Sarah stirred herself at last. "Why?"

"Why? Because we must. Because we always have."

A moan escaped from her. Her eyes were shut tight, but she seemed to be listening.

"Is Mottele still here?" she murmured.

Mottele ran to her and took her hand, holding it with both his hands, and she felt the boy's warmth.

"So you know how to kill, little brother," she murmured. "Congratulations."

"Come to the *budke* tonight, Sarah," Jacob began again. "I'll expect you there. And Misha would want you to hear with the others what the *haverim* have to endure in Warsaw, in Vilna, especially in Lodz, where I come from. Have you heard what happened to the 'Little Doctor'?"

Sarah turned, her eyes full on Jacob, wide awake now and fearful.

"They had raped him and his whole family, so the 'Little Doctor' became a partisan, a big rescuer of Jews. Well, the bastards killed him today near a German garrison. But first, Sarah, he took a lot of them with him."

12

Diadia Misha stood before his group commanders and the family-camp director in the *budke*. Moonbeams slanted through the window on the candlelit scene. Fastened on a wall near the fireplace was a multicolored icon, which featured a purple-robed Jesus surrounded by rapturous saints. Some motes swam around the icon, which was the only wall decoration. Mottele's violin case leaned against the wall under the sacred plaque.

On a few stools and on the floor, the men relaxed over mugs of coffee, some, Misha speculated, probably laced with vodka. They remained on alert, each man with his rifle or with an automatic in his belt.

"I'm taking time for this meeting," Misha began, "because many rumors are going around in camps and the ghettos. There's a rumor that the Allies have announced that all surviving Jews are to become their nationals after the war. There's another that Hitler is dying. There's another that peace is at hand, the enemy's being driven out by Russia. It's all rubbish! This is what's true: resistance is certainly growing in certain ghettos and labor camps, even though the people are starving and don't have weapons, and the Nazis are killing children and the old people."

His voice trembled. He adjusted his spectacles.

Mottele slipped into the room, and Misha threw him a welcoming nod. The boy took a seat next to Lyonka. He had come to listen, but he had come mostly with Sarah on his mind. He hoped fervently that Jacob had shaken her out of her deadly apathy. He missed her. Now he leaned forward, intent on Misha's briefing, accepted as one of the men.

"As most of us know, the central authority of the big-city ghettos is the Judenrat—the so-called Jewish Councils, appointed by the Germans to carry out their orders. Many Jews, especially the rabbis, I want our Gentile comrades to understand, felt bound to accept leadership posts on these councils. They hoped to be a buffer between their people and the German despots. They argued, perhaps rightly, that someone had to do the job—help people to get ration cards, a room to live in, jobs, medication, the sustaining things of life. People have to endure, to survive, they figured.

"But these Jewish elders differ from one another. Many are very brave men, very brave. Some have already been shot to death for trying to help the underground, or refusing to deliver up Jews to the Germans. Then there are the other kind," he continued in a flat tone, "both leaders and Jewish Police. The Germans dress up the Jewish Police in uniforms and shiny boots and official caps—*and* the Star of David on the uniform. They are mostly picked, I suppose, because they have no scruples. Well, this type isn't peculiar to the ghettos; it comes in all shapes and sizes of the human race," he enunciated dryly, "as partisans well know. In a way the Jewish Police have become the real tragedians in their peculiar human comedy, as I'll tell you."

Misha paused to drink some coffee. No one stirred. It had been a long time since anyone had brought them information about the outside world. Their days were mainly days of slogging through forest trails, planting mines, doing the ordered sabotage, plundering a train for equipment, killing with no remorse, improvising to stay alive, improvising to find the way "home," resting a bit before the next mission, which could come on the same day. This heavy-set, scholarly, bespectacled man clearly had no illusions that their engagements with the enemy would decide the future of the world. But he did affirm life, and he did have a broad perception of their particular hell. Now he was orchestrating the pattern of their days, of war and resistance, but in human terms that stretched their minds beyond the confines of camp and forest and missions. And they strained, Gentile and Jew, to follow Misha to some understanding.

"The Nazi liquidation of the Warsaw ghetto has already begun," Misha went on. "Hundreds of thousands of Jews have been deported—killed—from that ghetto alone. The irony is this: I've learned that the latest *Aktion* included the Jewish Police and their families. As you see, collaborators aren't exempt . . . they're just Jews."

Misha removed his glasses, and used his fist to wipe the sweat off his brow. He looked at his silent commanders. Genocide was hardly unknown to them. Each one had a private torment. But, he argued inwardly, the Jewish torment was surely the greatest, the worst on earth. He was suddenly aware of Sarah, standing in the door of the wooden hut.

She had washed herself, flattened the wild, curling hair; she was wearing a boy's clean work shirt and trousers, the cuffs tucked into the tops of her short boots. Her dark-ringed eyes, enormous and frightened, seemed to pierce her pinched face. She was staring uncertainly over the heads of the roomful of men, seeking Misha and his invitation to enter. Misha felt an immense pity for the girl flood over him, but he sent her only a silent, encouraging nod. The others followed his example, routinely receiving the girl like any comrade. Misha went on quietly.

"You know about Dr. Atlas, the great partisan leader who was killed today. He came from the town of Lodz, and the story of Lodz is so strange and complex that I want you to hear it from a Lodz veteran. Jacob!"

Jacob got to his feet. He wondered how far he could go with this mixed company—how far he *should* go. It was one thing to tell it to fellow Jews, quite another to make the strange scenario credible to Gentiles. He decided to hold nothing back. How long had he been part of Uncle Misha's partisans anyway? Was it only three months since he'd managed to escape, crazed by grief, with his small son—only to give the child to Gentiles? Good God, to be able to retrace his way and bring his son to the family camp here!

Jacob couldn't start.

"Mottele!" Misha called, sensing some dilemma. "More coffee for everyone! Mottele, wake up. . . . Coffee!"

Mottele had been staring at Sarah, his heart pounding with happiness and relief, and his impulse had been to run to her. The men laughed as he stumbled to his feet. Their laughter broke the tension in the room, and Mottele joined in sheepishly.

"I'm sorry, Uncle Misha." The boy stepped gingerly over the men's legs to the wood stove, where the coffee was bubbling hot. He poured some into a smaller pot, and carried that around to replenish the men's mugs. He saw Sarah take his place, sitting very upright next to Lyonka, and he heard Lyonka murmur, "Shalom, Sarah."

She nodded stiffly. Her attention was riveted on Jacob.

"As Misha said, the Lodz story is very complex," Jacob began, returning Sarah's look with one that told the girl she was doing well. "It's difficult to understand, but I don't want to give you a whole *megillah*. . . ."

This won a small smile from Sarah and the Jewish partisans. "I'll deal with just the highlights. The Lodz story is very valid tonight for a couple of reasons. First, we've said Kaddish for our comrade Dr. Atlas, who was once connected with Lodz. Then, for a true memorial to Dr. Atlas, I thought, Misha thought, that his fighting spirit and sacrifice needed to be contrasted with another kind. The kind practiced by a very limited but powerful man who thinks he is the new King of the Jews!"

This time the Gentile partisans reacted, shifting uneasily.

"I'm sorry to remind you, Mottele," Jacob went on with great calm, singling the boy out, "that he carries the grand name of our Biblical wizard Mordechai . . . like you."

Mottele's name hadn't received the full treatment for a long time, and he laughed and, suddenly affecting the high singsong of a *cheder* lesson, he recited: "In Queen Esther's time, Mordechai prevented the persecution of the Jews by the wicked Haman!" He was showing off for Sarah, and she gave him a beautiful smile.

"That's my boy," Jacob said dryly. "But this one—his full name is Mordechai Chaim Rumkowski—is hardly a lovable old wizard. In fact, we call him the Jewish Führer." Jacob paused to let it sink in.

Mottele brought Sarah a mug of coffee, and his hand touched hers. She clasped his hand briefly as she took the nourishment, and he was filled with happiness. His chore finished, he came and sat at Sarah's feet.

"You should know something about Lodz before Rumkowski headed the Jewish Council," Jacob was continuing. "We had the best reservoir of skilled Jewish labor in Poland; in fact, Lodz is called the Manchester of Poland because of its textile factories and tanneries and skilled workers, and the Germans knew it and wanted this source of labor and supplies for the German Army. Well, Rumkowski is determined, believe this or not, to build what he calls 'a model ghetto,' to show what Jews are capable of! It's an obsession with him—his way, he says, of *saving* Jews. Work, he says, is our passport to being left in peace. The work, you understand, is for the Wehrmacht. He opposes *any* underground, *any* attempt to escape. Those who don't like his policy, or who can't work, sign their own death warrants. They go to the killing centers."

Jacob drank his coffee, and the partisans waited, murmuring disbelievingly. The yeshiva scholar went on, his voice toneless and hard. "The Germans have a great sense of drama. They made Rumkowski head up the Judenrat, the Jewish Council, we think because he looked the part—very distinguished with his white mane of hair and strong chin, and authoritative, like the Germans—but he also suited their ghetto purposes, *to use Jews to degrade other Jews.* That way they could prove their theory that Jews were subhumans. Psychologically a very interesting man, this Jewish Führer. When we called him to his face King Chaim, he took the insult as a compliment!"

Jacob paused again, and stared at the icon and at Mottele's fiddle. He was struck by the juxtaposition of such symbols of faith and culture in this savage corner of the world. He struggled with his memories as he turned back to the partisans.

"Rumkowski collaborates in this way with the head of the German Ghetto Administration, one Hans Biebow. The German and the Jew have got the factories working overtime in Lodz. They're filling orders from the Nazi armaments industry. To King Chaim, I repeat, it's simple arithmetic: resistance is impossible; the underground impossible. He actually believes he can set up an autonomous Jewish city-state eventually, called Lodz.

"Take what happened when some German administrators came on a visit to Lodz. They congratulated Biebow and Rumkowski for the work *their* Jews were doing for the German Army. But they asked why the Jewish judges didn't sentence to death those 'criminals' who listened to the Allied newscasts. Later Rumkowski ordered the judges to do that—impose the death sentence for such 'crimes'—and when the judges resigned rather than cooperate, he saw that they went on the death transports."

An awful silence now filled the room, and it seemed to Jacob that the Jewish partisans in particular were shaken by his briefing. Misha and Lyonka and Popov looked at him in dumb amazement, but his story seemed chiefly to stun the boy.

Mottele had got up to repeat his coffee chore, and he was conscious that Jacob was trying, not always successfully, to keep the account unemotional, to give the true, other side. But there was so much the boy couldn't understand. He thought about the exchange he'd had with Lyonka when they'd gone fishing, when he'd asked his friend why God had "let it happen." And Lyonka had replied, "It's not God, it's men." Remembering that exchange now left Mottele more puzzled than ever. Jewish men, too, then?

Mottele, filling the mugs, listened closely. Jacob's tone had suddenly softened. "The curious thing is—and I think this never failed to astonish the Jewish Führer—Hans Biebow liked to beat him up! Biebow makes a lot of profits from the factory production, but when he gets drunk, he likes to remind the King that he's just another Jew. Once he came to Rumkowski's office when he was drunk, and he beat Rumkowski so badly that the King had to be in the hospital for days!"

There were grim smiles all around on that one. The worst, the most wounding part of Jacob's story was yet to come. Jacob stared miserably at Mottele, sitting again at Sarah's feet, with Sarah's hand on the boy's shoulder. Lyonka, Sarah, Mottele—like a family sitting for a portrait. He *had* to tell about the children, and this hurt the most.

"The children," he began again, "were Rumkowski's special passion, his *kinderlach*. I don't want to spare anyone, certainly not myself. In the beginning, we *wanted* to believe in Rumkowski's theories. Lodz ghetto at least was alive, the people worked, they had bread. But then Rumkowski started on the children, including *his* orphans."

And, hardly audible now, Jacob recounted what he had told Jenya.

He was glad that Jenya had decided not to come. When he finished, he saw Mottele, very pale, get to his feet, as the room filled with angry mutterings from all sides. The boy's eyes, only moments before shining with love and happiness because of Sarah's presence, were blazing with his inner turmoil. Mottele was seeing his little sister, Batya, again, and his voice was suddenly louder than the rest, and his words were strange in his own ears as he cried out, "King *Chaim!* Don't you mean *Haman,* Jacob—Haman, the king of bastards?"

The boy had said it for all of them, and the room fell quiet under his furious outburst. Sarah drew him down gently and held his hand.

"Can't more people *fight* their way out, try to join the partisans?" someone asked insistently.

"Rumkowski doesn't want the Germans antagonized!" Jacob answered. "Anyone found going near the wire is shot to death. Me—I escaped by chance.

"My wife had been killed . . . dead of typhus. They said they suspected that my son and I were typhus carriers, so they put us on the transport for Chelmno, the killing center. We were placed with about twenty other Jews, and some dead people, on a flatbed truck. I was sitting on the edge, and my brain was completely empty. But I saw there were only four Germans, one in each corner of the truck, with submachine guns. I don't know what happened exactly, but we were now outside the ghetto and going through the city of Lodz, and there was a bump in the road or something, and that woke me up, threw me out of my lethargy.

"I looked around. The dead bodies were in the middle of the truck, and there were all of us, and there were those four Germans. I yelled, *'Yehudim! Yetz! Jews! Now!'* I held my son in one arm, and I grabbed a German around the neck, and the man next to me grabbed his gun. We kicked the German off the truck, and the man started shooting the Germans. Other prisoners grabbed their guns as they fell, and they fired through the window at the German driver. It was a fantastic feeling. We were all yelling. We were doing something!

"The truck crashed against some trees, and we scrambled the hell out. We left their bodies among the dead Jews, and ran for our lives. We were on the outskirts of Lodz now, near the woods, and some said they'd try to get to Warsaw. They didn't want to chance it in the forest, they said, because the enemy was all around there."

Jacob paused uneasily. He hadn't meant that to slip out, with Gentiles present, but his words didn't bother them.

"But why Warsaw, Jacob?"

"Transports are going from there every day, too, Jacob, didn't they know?"

"So why Warsaw?"

Jacob shrugged wearily. "Where else can Jews who fear the forest go in Poland?"

"Even though the Germans are killing the Warsaw population?"

"Even though. . . ."

Jacob waited for more questions, but an enormous silence pervaded the little hut again, each man with his own thoughts. The moonbeams had vanished. The forest outside was thickly blanketed by night, but indoors was a kind of Sabbath warmth, a close feeling of family. Coffee bubbled on the stove, and the fat candles on tabletops had burned low, but their light reflected on the colorful icon and on the violin case.

Mottele was glad of the quiet. His agitation had simmered down. He felt he had heard too much again, that his memories were too raked over, but at least in this quiet company, a full-fledged member of the forest fighters, he could feel at one with the best of people. He stared with fascination at the candles stuck in thick grease. The boy grew dreamy. He liked the way the people were bunched together in the hut, against their common enemies, and against the dark, too, that Sarah feared. He willed Jacob's words to recede. Now, with his beloved Sarah's hand in his, the moment was so fine that he thought, for her sake, he would have liked to break the solemnity all around them with some fast fiddle playing.

Instead he turned to Sarah, wanting to see her smile again, and whispered, "Someone who comes from Warsaw gave me a poem from a kid there who's called Mottele, too."

Sarah looked at him questioningly.

"Well, he thought I should have it because of our names. Want to hear how it goes?"

She nodded.

"It's a bit *meshugge.*"

Mottele got the smile.

"Well, it starts: 'From tomorrow on, I shall be sad—/ From tomorrow on!/ Today I will be gay./ What is the use of sadness —tell me that? . . .' "

"You should put that to music, Mottele."

"I think I'm going to."

Her hand stroked his hair. She turned to Lyonka.

"I haven't thanked you and Mottele for what you did."

"It's not important, Sarah."

"That's all over and done with," Mottele said.

"No, little brother," she said. Her eyes avoided his. She seemed to be miles away from them again. "But Jacob is right. We have to get on with . . . things."

"That's what the kid wrote."

"What kid?"

"The kid in Warsaw, in his poem. 'What's the use of sadness?' he wrote."

"It will make a lovely song, Mottele."

"I'll write it for you, Sarah."

"Thank you."

She was back with them again, smiling her old broad smile. Sarah turned to Lyonka, finding at last that she could look at him straight, studying the tough, thoughtful face of her lover without dread. Lyonka drew close to her, powerfully moved by what he saw in her face. Mottele, seeing the intimate look that went between them, was confused and hurt by it. He had a sudden impulse to throw himself between his two best friends. He would have liked to hold Sarah very hard, even in front of Lyonka and the others.

Jacob was still speaking, his voice parched, despite the coffee. Mottele twisted angrily back to listen.

"But *Warsaw* will resist. They have partisans inside the ghetto, and they'll fight. The German intention is to wipe out that biggest ghetto, and the Jews left there want to break out, but they can't. The ghetto is completely walled in. The people have no weapons. They're overwhelmed. And the outside world . . ."

Jacob's voice had risen, scornful, thundering suddenly like an Old Testament prophet: "The outside world doesn't give a damn whether that ghetto lives or dies! There's a war on! they say. But the Warsaw ghetto is trying to do something, and we know what *they're* saying—that they're going to give the Nazi bastards a run for their money! Warsaw is not Lodz!"

For they sow the wind, and they shall reap
the whirlwind . . .

HOSEA 8:7

13

In that violent summer of 1942, while the partisans, Jewish and
Gentile, tried to hold on to their few kilometers of forest, Adolf
Hitler seemed to be on the brink of achieving his mightiest goal
—conquering the world. General Rommel, the "desert fox,"
was doing havoc to British defenses with his Afrika Korps and
was already at El Alamein, close to British defenses in Egypt.
And on the Russian front, Germany's famous Sixth Army was
just north of Stalingrad.

So confident was Hitler that he had built a "Werewolf Headquarters" near Vinnitsa in the Ukraine—almost within spitting
distance of the forest partisans!

On their part, the Allies in the West were too weak to risk
opening a second front by crossing the English Channel in
order to challenge the Axis, which had already turned the Medi-
terranean into a blue Axis lake. And so the crucial months of
1942 were months of German victories. While Winston Churchill's strategy was being bitterly attacked in Parliament, Hitler
was gleefully telling his commanders that "Russia is finished."
In fact, the taking of Stalingrad became his obsession, a matter
of personal prestige, and he demanded that the great Russian
cities of Stalingrad, Leningrad, Moscow be leveled to the
ground. The Führer was so intent on his dream that he was now
personally directing the war from his Ukrainian headquarters,
scorning—screaming down—the warnings of his worried army
intelligence that Russia was far from finished, that his course
was dangerous for Germany. Ignoring the experts, he sent a
secret directive on July 23 to his commanders, which read:

In a campaign which has lasted little more than three weeks, the broad objectives outlined by me for the southern flank of the Eastern front have been largely achieved. . . . The early destruction of the city of Stalingrad is especially important.

Adolf Hitler

Russia's High Command intelligence had the gall to radio Hitler's directives to all its fighting units, including the partisans. But the news of most interest to the partisans was the Hitler directive of August 18, pointing directly to them. It said:

In recent months banditry in the East has assumed intolerable proportions. . . . By the beginning of winter these bandit gangs must be substantially exterminated, so that order may be restored behind the Eastern front, and severe disadvantages to our winter operations avoided.

This directive described to the German Armed Forces, the SS, the Chief of German Police, and the Commander in Chief of the Air Force just how the "bandits" were to be destroyed. The emphasis was to be on recruiting more native units of local people, so many of whom had already taken action against the "bandits."

The communiqués caused quite a flurry in the *budke* and the radio hut, and Jacob put translated excerpts into his little newspaper—which was now crested with a title, *To Freedom*—for the partisans had earned a secret directive from Hitler himself.

Mottele, helping Jacob with the translations, was duly impressed.

"He's got his headquarters right near us!" he exploded. "And here's the evidence, Jacob, that they're recruiting local people to help them."

"You needed *more* evidence?" retorted Jacob. "You've forgotten the butcher, maybe, and that lot?"

"Some people will call this lies anyway."

"Some people."

In the radio hut, where Jacob printed in Yiddish and Mottele in Ukrainian, the two friends worked rapidly, man and boy glad of the quiet together and the respite. Their lead pencils made an occasional counterpoint on the lined copybook paper.

"Listen, Mottele, I have an idea," Jacob said suddenly. "What do you say we add, in this issue, that poem from the Warsaw lad you're putting to music? Make a nice contrast with this Hitler garbage, don't you think?"

"Some *shiddach*, marrying those two!" Mottele said with a laugh. "But why not? I know the poem by heart." And he began to write it down.

He would have loved, he told himself as he printed the poem and Jacob copied it in Yiddish, to have known his namesake. The Warsaw boy wrote so simply and defiantly. He wondered if the boy still lived, or if he'd been sent on a transport.

> From tomorrow on, I shall be sad—
> From tomorrow on!
> Today I will be gay.
>
> What is the use of sadness—tell me that?
> Because these evil winds begin to blow?
> Why should I grieve for tomorrow—today?
> Tomorrow may be so good, so sunny,
> Tomorrow the sun may shine for us again;
> We shall no longer need to be sad.
>
> From tomorrow on, I shall be sad—
> From tomorrow on!
> Not today, no! Today I will be glad.
> And every day, no matter how bitter it be,
> I will say:
>
> From tomorrow on, I shall be sad,
> Not today!

The poem had no title, and he now gave it one: "Mottele's Song, from Warsaw."

They threw down their pencils, tired but very pleased with their joint work. This paper would certainly be a unique issue. The Hitler directives were absorbing and proved that the Russian High Command was intercepting and breaking the Nazi codes. The Jewish stuff made a good balance. Jacob had an afterthought, and started to add another paragraph. He read it to Mottele, who nodded with appreciation as he copied it in his round, precise hand.

The story is being told that people are criticizing Churchill's handling of the war, and his policies. We have it on high authority that Mr. Churchill is not amused by this, especially when they say, "It's about time the British Lion showed its teeth." He always replies: "Not before the Lion has gone to the dentist!"

Gallows humor, maybe, but of the sort that implied that all was far from lost, thought Jacob, as he got up to stretch. He poured mugs of coffee for Mottele and himself, dropped a lump of sugar into each, and told the boy, "Jenya is bringing our lunch over today."

Mottele sat back and regarded his friend with interest and not a little shyness. "Can I ask you something, Jacob?" he asked. "You in love with Jenya?"

"What's that?"

"Uh—in love with Jenya?"

"Well, I don't know. I love all of you, little brother—Jenya, Misha, Sarah, Lyonka, Ivan. . . ."

"That's not the same."

"Same as what, Mottele?"

"Well, you know, the same as . . . being *in* love. With Jenya," the boy said doggedly. "Are you going to marry her?"

"Jenya is just a very good and very kind . . . friend."

"And that's all?"

"No," said Jacob, with his patient smile, "but that's all you'll get out of me."

"But every time you return from a mission you go straight to Jenya, don't you, Jacob?"

"Yes."

"So then you love her, don't you? I mean in a special way, different from Lyonka and me?"

The man hesitated. "This is important to you, Mottele?"

"Yes, it's very important."

"Then listen to me, little rabbi," Jacob said softly. "I don't think in those terms, not yet anyway. I've lost everything and everyone I loved truly in the old life, and this forest life is still new to me, but most of all I'm wondering all the time about my . . . my way to God. Curiously enough, I find that I'm wrestling not with the question of love, but the question of guilt. Why was I saved? Why?" And in the moment the yeshiva scholar seemed to have forgotten Mottele, seemed to be praying in the synagogue or *cheder, davening* but without the rocking movements. "I think that the image of God is in danger. The shadow of Cain is on the face of mankind, and it's fallen over the image of God, whose Word we keep in our hearts. Many generations to come, and not just of Jews, will have to live with what is happening now to us, the Jews. The mark of Cain which is blurring the image and the Word must never be forgotten. We can forgive in time, yes, but only if *they* won't forget.

"The Kaddish affirms faith. It's not a prayer for the dead alone, which is what it appears to be, but it's our affirmation— our song, affirming life and faith and grandeur. But we have to ask ourselves: faith in *what* today? In goodness, in love, in God? How can you talk about God? you may ask. And I have asked it myself: How can you believe in God? But if I am to affirm life, the question really is: How can you *not* believe in God? Each morning we rise and say, 'Thank you, God, for returning to me my soul, which was in Your keeping.' So we have been taught through the ages. So how can you *not* believe in God? I ask. All the same I feel the guilt. And I wonder, Where is God?

"We Jews are as quick to self-blame as to self-praise. Does that account for the guilt? Is that what sustains us? My teacher used to say jokingly, 'If Moses couldn't get along with the Jews, how can the man in the street?' We're such a stiff-necked people. For me it always comes back to the question: Why was *I* saved? Why were my loved ones taken . . . and all the others? I know that at least here we're acting. We, at least, are doing something. Still I feel the guilt. . . ."

Jacob stopped suddenly, the agony showing in his face, which was like a battleground of emotions, his gaunt features at war with themselves. And the boy, reacting to Jacob's sensitivity, was very pleased that his friend was talking to him man to man, though he couldn't follow all of it; he knew he should probably stop, but he kept at Jacob, wanting answers.

"You said before that you loved all of us," the boy began again, "Misha, Lyonka, Sarah, Jenya. . . ."

"And so I do."

"Then what do you mean that you can't love *truly* now?"

"Ah, I was talking about the old kind of love, lad, between husband and wife, and father and son; the . . . binding kind, Mottele."

Jacob fell into a brooding silence, but the boy pressed on, wondering why Jacob was confusing love with guilt. He wanted to understand. "Lyonka says we have to go on loving, and he *meant* the . . . the binding kind."

"So that's Lyonka."

"Don't you agree, then?" Mottele asked.

"I'm a bit older than both of you, so let's say that makes me skeptical."

"You're laughing at me now."

"Come on, Mottele, what's *really* on your mind?"

"I just wondered."

"*You* in love with someone, little rabbi?"

Mottele blushed, and his head went down.

"I'll bet it's little Mirel—is that it, Mottele?"

"Now you're being stupid!" the boy flared up. "She's just a child!"

Jacob gave a shout of laughter at that. He grabbed Mottele, hugged him, and his laughter was such a release, and so good to hear, that the boy joined in. Then as suddenly, Jacob, the scholar and philosopher, so rocklike and stubborn, did a strange thing.

He sat down at the table, where they had worked on the new issue of *To Freedom,* and buried his head in his arms and he wept. Mottele sat beside Jacob, not knowing what to do.

"Stop crying, Jacob," he whispered. "Please stop!"

The man stood up. He went to stand at the window, drying his eyes on his shirt sleeve. The sun was shining and the trees with their thick foliage looked rosy pink under streamers of light, but inside, the hut seemed burdened with heavy shadows. Mottele wanted to go to his friend, but he hesitated.

A moment after, the door opened, letting in a draft of cold, bracing air, a herald of the freezing weather to come. Jenya made a pretty sight, with her hair pushed into a bright babushka, a printed apron over her rough, woolly skirt, carrying in their hot lunches of sausage, boiled potatoes and beets. She stopped for a moment, looking at Jacob; then she put down the lunches on the table and went to stand beside him, her hand on his shoulder.

"Come on, you two, eat up while it's hot."

Jacob looked at her.

"Come on. Eat it while it's hot," she commanded gently.

Misha was wrong about one rumor, and he was the first to admit this, joyously.

The war was really beginning to turn in their favor.

It began late that year, when the whole of the Ukraine and Byelorussia and the Eastern front were blanketed with snow, piled with snowdrifts in a regular freezing Russian winter—and it was weather, the historic enemy of invaders, that began to defeat the German invaders.

Both Nazis and partisans were immobilized by the weather, which, starting routinely in late summer, developed brutal temperatures that fell below zero. The enemy was not equipped to meet this, and the summer of 1942, which had so elated Hitler, soon was veering into his savage winter of despair. Soviet aircraft, flying above the enemy lines, dropped the news about this into partisan camps. The biggest turning point came on all fronts—in November 1942. By then, under General Eisenhower, Anglo-American troops were hitting the beaches of North Africa . . . were in Morocco and Algeria. . . .

The Americans were attacking Japanese forces at Guadalcanal. . . . Britain's Eighth Army was beating the "desert fox," winning victories at El Alamein and spelling General Rommel's doom. . . . On the Eastern front, Germany's famous Sixth Army, following Hitler's order to keep hammering at Stalingrad, found itself between the Don and the Volga—trapped by seemingly endless thousands of Russian soldiers.

Misha and his brigade were certain now: The whole balance of military power was shifting, and the war's initiative was suddenly in Allied hands.

The British Lion had been to the dentist!

That month of November, Hitler left for his Alpine haven in Berchtesgaden, where he was wont to consult astrologers and, it was rumored, the gods. His idyllic dream of leveling Russian cities was being nastily shattered. The Russians had launched a counteroffensive in a blizzard and Germans were about to beat an unscheduled retreat from Stalingrad; in fact, the Russian winter was driving Hitler's troops nearly insane, and the whole of his Sixth Army was starving and wanted to surrender. Hitler ranted, in an extraordinary directive to his commanders: "Surrender is forbidden! Sixth Army will hold their positions to the last man and the last round!"

In the Ukraine, the partisans, whom Hitler called the *Untermenschen*—subhumans, to be exterminated by his master Nordic race—had waited for this moment. The war was far from over, but Hitler's "Werewolf Headquarters" lay in ruins, and radio reports documented the Allied push on all fronts. Diadia Misha and his brigade decided on a celebration, their first as a joint command. It took place in the family camp.

The mothers and old ones had strung up banners across the trees—WELCOME, PARTISANS! GOD BLESS YOU! SHALOM! The family camp was primarily Jewish, with some hundred members, and they turned the occasion into an *Oneg Shabbes*. By some miracle, the women had baked the traditional *challahs*, and on long tables in their "meeting house," which doubled as school and synagogue, the braided loaves of bread were ceremoniously spaced between plates of salami and herrings and small cakes and bottles of wine and the great favorite, kvass.

But first some Jewish partisans, rifles beside them, joined the old *tsaddiks,* who fingered their phylacteries and fringed *talliths,* and prayed with them: "Blessed art Thou, the Eternal, our God, King of the Universe, who hath preserved us alive, sustained us, and caused us to attain this season!" Then they all, Gentile and Jew, helped themselves to the festive foods. Mottele was to remember that they seemed like a great family welcoming in the Sabbath, the way his father would chant to Mama and Mottele and little Batya—the welcome to ministering angels: "May you bless us with peace, and may you depart in peace!"

Mottele had brought his fiddle. This night was for the old, well-loved songs, and he played everything they asked for— Ukrainian folk songs, sentimental Russian love songs, Yiddish songs learned from Jacob and Misha, Paderewski's "Minuet." He played the beloved Succoth harvest song:

> Why the *succah,* my father?
> The *succah* is to sit in, my dear boy!
> Why sit in there, good father?
> Our fathers also sat there, my dear boy. . . .

And he played the *Hatikvah,* the "national anthem" of Zionist meetings everywhere:

> We have never lost our hope,
> The hope to be a free people
> In the land of Zion and Jerusalem!

Then he went into a rousing hora. The people recognized it and started to push the tables to one side, and the dance began with, at first, a small, hesitant group. Then Jacob demonstrated the steps to those who had never danced the hora, and the circle grew wider and wider. The dancers grabbed one another's hands, and Mottele stepped up the beat as the dancers laughed and sang with his fiddle. The beat became more abandoned until, with Mottele fiddling wildly, the dancing circle filled the whole room, and even Misha joined the circle. Lyonka and Sarah, Jacob and Jenya, all in the big circle now, holding hands, forgetting everything else. For the moment.

The smallest children dashed inside the big circle and formed a smaller one of their own. Now the two wildly dancing circles were going in different directions. Mottele bowed away, faster and faster, feeling that he really needed the crashing of cymbals and tambourines to support his fiddle. He felt he was bringing literally to life the old Hebrew word for dance, meaning "to leap like lambs!" The whole room was really jumping, twisting, leaping. The hora was something he could keep going forever!

But even Mottele was exhausted at last. He finished it off with a big flourish, and the dancers fell apart, laughing and sweating. They loudly applauded their fiddler, and went to the tables, and toasted themselves and Mottele with raised glasses.

Sarah came and brought him a glass of wine.

"For my little genius," she said, smiling. She started to kiss him on the cheek, but impulsively he pulled her head down and kissed her on the mouth, hard. She stepped back then, puzzled but smiling still.

"I don't care, I love you, Sarah!" the boy blurted out. He looked both abashed and defiant.

"And I love you, little brother," said Sarah. She studied the boy for a moment, then, deliberately, she bent down and kissed him on the mouth. When she straightened up, she saw Lyonka and Jacob coming over. She moved to meet them, but changed her mind and gestured to them to stay away for the moment. She went back to Mottele.

For the rest of that evening, she stayed near him.

I am escaped with the skin of my teeth.
JOB 19:20

14

The full fury of the Russian winter now attacked Misha's camp. The howling of wolves day and night was as clear in the distance as the howling of angry winds close by, winds that lathered the trees with driven snow and piled up immense drifts. All the huts were buried in snow to their eaves. And except for the radio, tended like a sacred trust, the camp was cut off from the outside world. A few trails had been shoveled out or tramped down, but the snow soon covered them again. The great whitened forest looked monstrously disabled, muzzled by the relentless, nonhuman foe. But for the partisans, the forest, white or green, remained their best friend.

In fact, Misha had the partisans bury themselves, for further protection, under the crustaceous ground, for despite freezing temperatures, some Germans were still wandering through the forest. They either had been cut off from their units or, following the Hitler directives, were searching for partisans. So Misha ordered every able-bodied person to dig tunnels which would connect the fighters' compound to the family camp, and, from there, to the watchtowers at the edge of camp.

Everyone kept at this work for the tunnels also provided more storage for food, medical supplies, weapons. And despite the awful isolation, camp morale kept lifting in the bitter season, because they heard the war was turning.

Every week now, optimistic reports came over the radio about villages and towns being liberated by the Allied armies. From Moscow Radio itself, orders went to all partisan units—

coinciding, as it happened, with Misha's ambitions—to continue their sabotage, but also to make contact when possible with the Red Army. This would not only put them under an organized military command, but would also bring an end to the arduous forest life for the family-camp units, since the Red Army had orders to evacuate the families to the rear.

Also, a Russian plane had found Misha's camp, and often now a small group of partisans went through the tunnels to a prearranged spot where the plane was expected; it dropped supplies, guns, ammunition by parachute, and batches of leaflets from the Partisan High Command in Moscow. The one-page leaflets were as eagerly sought as the supplies, for they told the partisans about war developments, and gave them advice concerning enemy patrols in their area.

And always before flying off, the plane dipped smartly in salute. To the more religious of the partisans, the plane seemed sent straight from heaven. Once when Misha accompanied the group to watch the parachute drop, he laughed at the plane's farewell gesture, and gave it a smart hand salute back.

"Why not straight from heaven?" he exclaimed to Jacob on the return trip. "That pilot's close enough to Chelm on the border," he went on with a straight face. Jacob grinned expectantly.

Just the mention of the town of Chelm, with its mythical folk tales of endearing wise men and endearing fools, was guaranteed to make one react, for some story was bound to follow.

"Nu, Misha, I'm waiting!"

"Well, that plane up there, and us waiting anxiously for it down here, reminds me of this holy man from Chelm. He was told to go and sit on a high hilltop and wait for the Messiah to come. For a very long time he sat on the hilltop, and no one below knew what was going on. Then one day he came down again to Chelm. The people gathered around him. They had great respect for him, and they waited patiently, until one of them got up the courage to ask: 'So tell us, *Rebbe,* when is the Messiah coming? And what is it like up there?' The holy man thought it over, and took his time, and finally he replied: 'Well,

I'll tell you, it's like this. Up there, the pay is not so good, and it's lonely. But at least it's permanent!' "

Jacob burst into laughter.

But when he calmed down, his expression suddenly changed. "You think this condition of ours, Misha, is permanent?"

"No," replied Misha. But his smile was gone, too.

Late one January evening of the new year, when the ground lay frozen but firm enough for a march, Misha led several partisans to the edge of camp; among them were his son, Lyonka, Jacob, and Popov the engineer. They were muffled to their eyes, and each man carried along with his rifle a small bundle of rags. The men leaned their rifles against the trees and built a fire. They stood close together as they warmed themselves and waited for Diadia Misha's orders. The coming mission weighed heavily on Misha, but he spoke to the partisans in a crisp military tone to cover his worry.

"Comrades, I've brought you here because we have orders from Moscow concerning an armored train with twenty cars on its way to Kursk. Sometime last night, the train should have passed through Shepetovka. And this night around midnight or early tomorrow morning, it should be near Semigorod. Now, at an intersection near Semigorod, this train must hit a mine, which I want you to place. Popov has been briefed on the general area. You should also know that every partisan unit operating near this railway has been alerted, and has its own mission. We dare not miss. Here's why."

Misha looked at the fire and then at his men, keeping his voice very even. "On that train are three or four hundred German pilots. They have recently graduated from the pilots' school in Munich, and are traveling to Kursk airdrome, to take over the war planes waiting for them. Those planes are supposed to fly over and drop bombs on Moscow and Leningrad. So that's the picture."

There was a hush on the group as Misha paused, and Lyonka threw some dry branches on the fire. The pines and birches, against which their rifles leaned, were masked in snow and the trees seemed to bend over the partisans like eager eavesdroppers. The wind had stopped most of its torment, but the howling of wolves kept on in the distance.

"I want co-commanders on this mission," said Misha, handing Popov a marked sketch of their destination; the target—the bridge over which the train had to pass—was circled in black. "Popov will supervise the mine-laying under this bridge. And Jacob will coordinate the bombing action and the retreat. They may have to improvise, of course, depending on the train and the weather. Follow their instructions implicitly. One more thing: before you get to the junction, each man is to tie the rags around the soles and over his boots; that way you'll leave no footprints on the ground should the Germans pursue you after the derailment. Understood?

"Comrades," he went on, looking into each man's face, lingering a moment longer on Lyonka's, "this is our biggest sabotage assignment. The stakes are very high. Be careful. Do not think about heroics or death. Think only of vengeance against the enemy! Do as Popov and Jacob tell you. This mission must not fail. Now, prepare to be on your way. I have another mission to get off, back in camp. I want to see you all here by morning! Good luck!"

The partisans in the communications hut meanwhile waited for Misha. They knew about the bridge mission; both radio and field phone were momentarily silent while tension built. The men talked little. They smoked hand-rolled cigarettes, drank black coffee and waited.

Mottele came up into the hut from his underground bunker, which he shared with Lyonka and Jacob. Like the others, he was dressed for action in his cut-down khakis, his heavy leather belt, into which his gun was stuck, boots and muffler. No one in camp ever moved without his rifle or gun; in the family camp, people had stockpiled heavy stones, for despite the ammunition drops, the camp was short of defense supplies.

This was to be another main foray, but *after* Misha had gotten off the Popov-Jacob train mission. The plan was to ambush wandering Germans who could furnish them with the crucially needed military hardware.

The big wind, scouring the forest and sweeping fresh drifts against the hut, worked impartially against both partisans and enemy, but at least the partisans knew their Russian winters and were psychologically trained to endure them, but could the same be said of the Germans? It had been weather as well as Russian resistance that had managed to defeat Napoleon over a hundred years earlier, as every partisan, if not Hitler, well remembered; so the partisans rarely cursed the weather—they could wait. And meantime organize ambushes.

The door of the hut was flung open, and Misha came in.

"What's this—you here, too, Mottele?" Misha asked with surprise.

Mottele ran to fasten the door behind Misha. He was so thankful to see the "old man" that he felt like giving him a hug; instead he gave him an impudent salute. Misha smiled in return as he pulled off his greatcoat.

"Some coffee, Mottele?"

"There's hot cabbage soup, Diadia Misha."

"All right, lad. I'm famished."

"We're in luck, comrades," Misha said over the thick and steaming soup. "After I got the men off and started back home, I very nearly ran into a whole damn German convoy—it was on the road that splits the forest. Fortunately, the wind was kicking up such a snowstorm it hid me from their view. That storm—it's like a fantastic white shroud! I've never seen anything like it!"

"Their shroud, Diadia Misha," said Mottele confidently, taking away the empty soup bowl and bringing Misha some coffee. Misha held the mug tight, savoring its warmth, while he tried to calculate how far along the train mission might be.

"That convoy, Misha?" someone asked.

"Where's it now, do you think?"

"How big, Misha?"

"Cars or tanks?"

"Merciful Mother, have a heart, comrades!" Sergei cried.

"Give the old Cossack time to warm up!"

Misha nodded appreciatively, but the one thing they didn't have to spare that night was time. "Yes, I saw tanks, so this is one unit probably in full retreat," he went on. "We can't use rifles against tanks, but we can go after the bastards in the rear. I saw a couple of staff cars back there, and some individual soldiers stumbling around, looking like frozen snowmen. My God, they seemed tired. They couldn't keep up with the rest." He sounded strangely sad. Then, annoyed with himself, Misha threw off the mood. "But those staff cars looked like plenty of men and ammunition for us, comrades. Our target for tonight! Let's move!"

"Wouldn't you like to rest a bit, Misha?"

"What I'd like," Misha retorted, "is a warm inn, with my feet up on heated bricks, and a hot samovar in front of me, and a roaring fire, and twenty books! What we've got is a snowstorm and Germans! So let's move out, comrades!"

He got up and pulled his coat back on, and the others readied themselves to leave. Misha stared at Mottele's preparations.

But the boy looked straight at him with such stubbornness, as he adjusted his gun and muffler, that Misha could only shake his head and laugh; and he swallowed his intention to leave the boy in camp.

"All right, Mottele, but stay at the back with Sergei and do exactly as he tells you. Now, everyone, no straggling. And be careful!"

Just before the unit left, the radio began to chatter, and the men paused to listen. It was a communiqué from the Partisan High Command, relaying a warning about the German convoy in their area and "some more venom from the German Führer himself—that the fight against banditry is as much a matter of strategy as the fight against the enemy at the front."

Then with a nice touch of irony, the Russian voice continued: "The Nazi dictator warns, and I am quoting him, 'There must be no German in the area threatened by bandits who is not

engaged, actively or passively, in the fight against them.' End
of quote. Partisans! Keep up your attacks and sabotage! You can
see how your strategy threatens the enemy! We commend your
valor! Carry on!"

Hast thou found me, O mine enemy?

I KINGS 21:20

15

The men were chilled to the marrow, but Misha, leading the way, was grateful that the noisy wind covered their movement. They bent almost double against the gale's force; and the snow-laden trees, too, bent down and sighed like old men. It took nearly an hour before the partisans could make out their destination: a broad ribbon of road cutting through the trees, and on the road some of the heaviest military hardware Misha and his partisans had ever seen.

The men stole up to the edge of the forest and sat down to watch. The convoy seemed never-ending: tank after tank, armored cars, lorries of heavily armed soldiers, passing before their eyes as though on parade. The entire area hummed with the military activity. At last it began thinning out, and the parade was almost over when, separated from the rest of the convoy, a lorry came into view carrying officers and a few soldiers.

"That'll be our target—the lorry," ordered Misha. "Sergei, Mottele—stay behind and give us cover!"

As the target vehicle approached, Misha threw his grenade first, and the partisans simultaneously opened fire and charged. The lorry stopped, and the partisans rushed upon it. From the rear of the long motor truck, a machine gun began to rattle wildly, but the rest of the convoy had traveled too far ahead to notice the sudden tumult, and Misha's partisans were on the Germans before the machine gunner could take proper aim. A couple of partisans were grazed by bullets, but they managed to pull the soldiers off the lorry, and then they used their bayonets on them. The driver was already dead. Misha was finishing off a wounded German when he saw an officer run from the front seat. He brought the man down with a shot, and then he ran over to make sure the wounded officer wouldn't get away.

Just as Misha got to the man, the Nazi turned on his side to reach for his automatic, but Misha kicked the gun out of his hand. The Nazi raised himself to look at his tormentor, and Misha suddenly found himself staring into the face of the Gestapo commander of ghetto Korets! The handsome blond SS officer who had organized the mass-murder *Aktions* that had wiped out the Jews, and had stood over the survivors the day he ordered them to dig a mass grave.

"You, you goddamn bastard!"

Misha had often wondered what he would do if he ever caught up with this particular Nazi. For one mad second, Misha wished he could take him alive. The man was still staring into Misha's face, unrecognizing, hard, unflinching, contemptuous. He knew what to expect, and he tried to spit.

Without another word, Misha emptied his gun into the man. Then he bent down and stripped the dead Nazi of his gun, insignia ribbons and flask. With the toe of his boot, he shoved the man over on his face. To his amazement, Misha found that he had no feeling—it was, he said later, like killing a cockroach.

The whole episode had been swift, but now a couple of cars from the convoy had turned, and were coming back to find the lorry. Misha had started to run toward his unit when a final burst of fire came suddenly from the ambushed lorry, and he felt a bullet tear at his arm. He kept running, but it was difficult, and he stumbled and fell.

"Go on!" Misha yelled to the others. "I can make it all right! Get back!"

He began to crawl to the side of the road, toward the forest, conscious that the German cars were coming closer. Then he saw Mottele and Sergei, zigzagging their way between the trees at the road's edge and coming toward him. Mottele reached him just as the Nazis opened fire, and the boy used his gun to reply. Sergei threw a grenade on the Nazis, and other partisans kept giving covering fire as Mottele and Sergei helped to drag Misha back into the forest.

"Good lads! Help me stand up!"

"We have to run for it, Misha!" the boy urged.

"Right—let's run, then!"

The Germans had turned on their headlights and were firing from their cars, but evidently they feared to enter the dark woods against an unknown force, and they drove away to rejoin the convoy.

The partisans ran and slid their way into the icy undergrowth until they were out of firing range, and lay quite still, waiting to be sure the cars were gone. Then they took stock of their night's work: four machine guns, some rifles, ammunition; a dozen Nazis killed; a few coats, some warm furred hats and gloves; a convoy partially disrupted; a Gestapo commander killed. Not bad.

As for themselves, three men had superficial wounds; but Misha was losing blood from his arm. Sergei tore off his muffler and made it into a tourniquet to check the bleeding; he stuck a thick twig into the knot and twisted it to tighten the tourniquet. Misha winced with pain, but the first aid seemed to help.

The wind had died down and the trees had stopped their grumbling. The success of their daring ambush buoyed up each of them; and Misha, leading the way back to camp, still overwhelmed by his strange appointment with the SS man and death, felt elated. Above all, he thought as he and his men wearily reached camp when daylight was breaking, above all he could report to his son and Sarah and Jenya how he had avenged the deaths of their loved ones in Korets.

Each was busy with his own thoughts, but everyone was wondering, too, how the train mission had gone. In the communications hut, they warmed up, and drank hot coffee, and waited.

The waiting grew unbearable.

Sarah and Jenya and Ivan came to tend the wounded. They prepared a hot meal, made more coffee, drank vodka from the

Germans' flasks with the others, listened to the occasional radio reports; but nothing came over about the train mission. All day they waited for some word. The men slept little, but cleaned their guns and busied themselves, sweating out the frustration. They found, as time went by, that they were talking to each other in low tones, their elation over their own mission eroded by the awful anxiety, but most of the time there was silence in the hut.

Sarah had forced Mottele to get out of his heavy clothes and try to sleep; and the boy did indeed lie down on a cot for a moment, "just to rest, Sarah," He slept deeply for a couple of hours. When he awoke, Sarah and Jenya were gone, and some of the partisans were asleep; but Misha stood at the window, staring into the forest as though trying to penetrate its snow-bound secret. Mottele got dressed.

They waited the whole day, and twilight came early. Temperatures outside had dropped cruelly again, but the stove's fire had been built up, keeping the hut snug and warm. In anticipation of what? Mottele wondered miserably, with a shiver despite the warmth.

At last Sergei burst out, "Why the bloody hell don't they come?"

"They'll come," Misha said firmly.

"If they stay out there another night, they'll freeze to death!"

"They'll get here."

"So you hope!"

"So I hope," Misha said in a steady tone.

"It'll be a miracle, Misha, it'll have to be a miracle!"

"No miracle. Just take it easy, son. They'll get here!"

"Goddammit, the snow's starting again!"

"You want to go after them, Sergei?" Misha's voice had risen irritably.

"No."

"Then shut up, Sergei—please!"

The others listened painfully. Sergei was talking for all of them. They had themselves escaped by the skin of their teeth, beating the return of the Nazi convoy by minutes and luck; how much harder had it gone with the train saboteurs, now still out there in the frozen expanse? True, they were all professionals, but they were so few against so many. Had they succeeded? Had they lost their way back? Were they dead?

Mottele looked at Misha, and the boy knew Misha was afraid, too. He felt the tears start then, but forced them back. His head grew heavy, and he took off his belt and gun again, putting them near his violin, and slowly went to stretch out on top of the wood stove. He just wanted to stay warm, he told himself, and stop thinking. He fell asleep at once. He was still asleep when Sarah and Jenya, coming out of their bunker, saw the thin line of men moving toward camp. The girls ran to the communications hut, their faces radiant with happiness.

"Misha, it's them!"

"They're coming, they're all right!"

"Mottele, get up, little brother! I must build up the stove again!" Sarah cried.

Misha stood in the doorway as the men came closer, his face creasing with the dread of recognition: there were only five men, not six.

Exhausted and moving stiffly, the men came in. They nodded wearily, said a "Shalom" or two, and stumbled to the stove, or threw themselves on the floor and the cots.

"Shalom, Lyonka . . . Popov . . ." Misha began.

Jenya stood rigidly and felt her terror growing as she looked at the group and asked, "Where's Jacob?"

Lyonka could only shake his head, unable at first to say the words, then closing his eyes to close out his grief. "Jacob's dead. We had to leave him behind."

No one moved in the hut. Jenya's hand went to her mouth, and she remained where she stood, transfixed with horror and disbelief. The saboteurs sat in silence in their coats, not wanting to look at Jenya or Sarah or one another. Ivan limped around and poured each man some schnapps.

"We wanted to bring Jacob back with us, but we couldn't," Popov said quietly. "The mission had been a success, Misha, we were right on schedule. Then Jacob . . ." He stopped.

"Go on, Popov," said Misha.

"The train went up with every German on it. I think we got them all. I thought the whole goddamn horizon was on fire as the train went up." He paused, and looked toward Mottele with a wan smile. "It looked like Ovruch and the officers' club, Mottele, all over again."

Mottele could only stare at him. Popov's words were lost on the boy as he tried to take in the news about Jacob's death. Misha, seeing the boy's white, anguished face, said softly, "Get busy, lad, and pour some coffee for the men. Come on, I'll help you."

Mottele nodded, and mechanically he began to fill some mugs and hand them to Misha, who passed them around. Misha asked, "What happened, Popov?"

"It's been a strange night altogether, Misha. We laid the mines all right, and got back into a ravine and waited. We could see Germans patrolling the tracks—not many, but they had dogs with them. They probably had word that partisans, all along the route, had been waiting for this particular train. We were close enough to the patrol, but the Germans couldn't see us. Then the train came, and, like I said, everything was correctly timed, the mines went off when the cars were on the bridge . . . it was beautiful! There didn't seem to be any danger to us then. We had the rags on our boots and started to leave. We had a good head start. It was very dark, and the snow had started again. But we could hear the dogs barking—they'd got our scent—so we were hurrying, Jacob insisting on being last man out. The dogs were coming closer, but Jacob had ordered us not to use our guns, which could give our position away. The Germans were using theirs, though, as they came on with the damn dogs, and one of the shots got Jacob."

"How do you know he was dead!" Jenya's cry broke from her, filling the hut.

"He was quite dead, Jenya," Lyonka said, his head down. "We made sure." The silence in the room was unbearable, until Popov spoke up again. "There was no way we could bring Jacob back, Jenya. The Nazis were following us and we had to throw them off, stay away from the trails leading to camp, of course. Fortunately, they decided not to follow too deep into the forest, and after an hour or so they gave it up. That's why we're late, Misha; we were doubling in our tracks part of the time."

Popov drank his coffee and now there was a terrible silence in the room. Lyonka rose and pulled Sarah to him. She was sobbing helplessly, and the two stood closely huddled near the stove. Misha went to Jenya, but the girl fled out of the hut.

Misha watched her go. He felt very old and very angry. He had become immensely fond of the tall, abrasive yeshiva scholar, though he knew it didn't do to get too attached to any of his forest fighters. Dr. Atlas had wisely admonished, "You're only getting a reprieve from death—so you've just time to avenge yourself on the enemy." Misha repeated the advice to his own partisans, but just the same, he felt as if a limb had been torn from his body.

He turned back to the tired saboteurs and told them evenly, "Jacob's loss is a terrible blow. But we are—we must be—inured to such blows. There will be many more. You can be proud of the success of your mission, a very hard mission to carry out. You did well. He would want you to feel that way, too, men."

Mottele looked dumbly at the scene. He wouldn't give way like the girls, he told himself fiercely. But Jacob, his friend, was dead and he was very sick of death. He would miss Jacob very much.

He looked around the room, which he'd shared so often with his friend as they sat composing their camp newspaper. What was death like? What did Lamentations mean about "Reviver of the dead"? What could that *mean*—a call to the dead, a return to life, maybe?

"Jacob, why are you lying out there?" the boy raged inwardly. "Lying in some Godforsaken place where the dogs and birds can get at you? *Why? Why you?*"

His head hurt him, and he forced himself to go and stand near the radio, where the news was coming over. The boy tried to concentrate on it. Dimly he recognized one of their favorite foreign stations. It had always amused Jacob because it started off the same way each time, cheerfully, in the clipped English accents of the BBC: "This is London calling!"

Then routinely the voice went into a similarly brisk and cheerful precise translation in Russian: "This is London calling! Sending our greetings, and wishing the best of luck to our armed forces on the land, on the sea, in the air, and in our merchant navy!"

Mottele suddenly burst into a laugh—a grating, unexpectedly harsh laugh, as harsh as any grown man's. Full of contempt and despair. The men around Mottele looked up toward the boy, who stood like a statue with his back to them, staring at the radio.

The joy of our heart is ceased;
Our dance is turned into mourning.

LAMENTATIONS 5:15

16

Each of the partisans mourned Jacob's death in his own way.

To the Gentiles he had been an awesome symbol of ancient, spiritual resistance.

To the Jews, Jacob was the truest counterpart of the defenders of Masada—that stony cliff fortress above the Dead Sea in Palestine where, seventy years into the Christian era, a handful of valorous Jews resisted the overwhelming Roman armies. With no chance of victory against that enemy, the Jews nevertheless revolted against the oppressors, and died to the last man and woman rather than give in.

Each group remembered Jacob of Lodz. . . .

The Gentiles borrowed the radio hut for their memorial service. Mostly peasants and factory workers until they had turned partisans, they knelt down before the painted icon and fingered small crucifixes, or touched their heads to the ground in humility before God, and they implored of Him:

"Oh, Lord, rest among the saints the soul of your servant, Jacob of Lodz, where there is neither sorrow nor lamentation, but everlasting life."

"Eternal memory, eternal memory, eternal memory!" they chanted from the traditional funeral service.

Ivan led the chanting. He had difficulty in kneeling down and getting up again. His wounds had not healed properly; his left leg needed surgery and was almost useless. But he was far from immobilized, and helped to care for the horses, working in the kitchen as well.

Mottele, watching the Gentile service with polite detachment, was waiting to accompany Ivan back to the family camp. The big fellow loved the boy and worried about him. Mottele was altogether too contained, too stubbornly acting the man to give way to his real feelings.

As Ivan got up, Mottele wanted to go and help him to his feet, but he knew that would only make the man furious; instead he teased Ivan from the sidelines.

"So where's your crutch? What did we make it for if you don't use it?" Mottele demanded.

"And where's your manners, boy?" Ivan retorted. He smiled and started to pat the boy's head, but Mottele jerked away. He didn't want anyone to touch him. "You'll do for a substitute," Ivan went on, pretending not to notice. "Let's go!"

They headed over the frozen snow toward the family camp. There some old Jews were sitting *shivah* for Jacob, in the traditional seven days of mourning. Jacob was special, their Talmudist. They had ripped the lapels of their jackets in the ancient symbol of grief, and a *minyan* were finishing the Kaddish as Ivan and the boy arrived. One *bobeh* in the wooden hut had covered the small wall mirror ("Vanity of vanities, all is vanity"). And the old ones recited from the Talmud that loss is inevitable in life; they were not to mourn self-accusingly.

Because they knew what Jacob had meant to Jenya some of them had wanted to go to her, to comfort her and sit *shivah* with her, but Misha had restrained them. "She wants to handle this in her own way," he'd said. "Except you, Mottele. You go to Jenya. She said she'd like to have *you* with her."

The boy was grateful. The strange mystique of suffering and lamentation was having its effect on him. Vaguely he felt guilty about having missed the Kaddish; but something inside him wouldn't let him accept Jacob's death as final: Not until Jenya did, he told himself. On the way to Jenya's bunker, he found himself trying to remember Jacob's words when he said he was wrestling with his thoughts of love and guilt and God. ". . . shadow of Cain on the face of mankind . . . shadow over the image of God, whose Word we keep in our hearts."

The Jenya whom Mottele joined was not the Jenya of Korets. When the Nazis had killed her family, she had gone wild, tearing up everything around her, tearing her own flesh, trying to destroy the world the way it had destroyed them. Since then she had learned how to go on living, how to cope with the arduous forest life; even how to care for someone again. But this new loss was too overwhelming. It was so sudden, so violent and so mean that she felt widowed. As Mottele arrived, she imagined that Jacob had come in the door with him, for the boy had meant so much to Jacob.

"Shalom, Jenya." Mottele went to sit near her on the cot.

"Shalom, Mottele."

"Misha told me—"

"I asked him to let you come."

"I would have anyway, Jenya."

"I know."

"I wanted to talk with you about Jacob. Is it all right?"

"Go on, Mottele."

"I need to talk about him."

"I want you to, Mottele."

"It hurts, Jenya, but I need to."

"It's all right. It will help me, too."

But at first Mottele couldn't. She understood, and let him sit close to her but not touching, and for a while they sat that way in the dim crude little underground shelter, huddled against the unknown.

"You remember the day we celebrated with the dance in the family camp?" Mottele began again.

"I remember."

"A bit earlier, Jacob and I were working on the newspaper, the one with the Warsaw kid's poem in it."

Jenya nodded, recalling it well.

"When we finished that issue, we talked about a lot of things and—well, about you, Jenya."

"Yes, yes—tell me."

"He talked about you and about God, and . . . and death."

"Go on, little brother."

"I wanted to understand, so I kept after him." His throat felt very dry, but he persisted. "I just wanted to know if you can love someone, you know, in a . . . sacred way."

"*You* love someone that way, Mottele?" the girl asked thoughtfully.

"Well . . . yes."

"And that's the way you think Jacob loved me?"

"I think so."

"Did *he* tell you that?"

"Not exactly. He said he loved all of us—Misha, Sarah, Lyonka, Ivan, you . . . me. But I wanted him to talk about the special kind. Like when a person loves someone very passionately," he blurted out.

"I understand, Mottele," she said.

She looked at the boy, and wanted to touch him and console him, to cradle him. But that, she felt, would be too self-serving, no use to him at all in his solemn moment. So she told him in a practical tone, "Mottele, I think Jacob loved me very much, and I loved him. He always came to me after his missions. But he never used the words of love to me. I think he couldn't do that. I think one has to find new ways of saying emotional things after a terrible personal loss. For me it was enough that he wanted to come straight to me."

Mottele sat pondering her words as the girl fell quiet, and then she went on: "What else did you talk about?"

"I didn't understand all of it. He talked a lot about feeling guilty. He sounded like my teacher in *cheder*, Jenya. He said he was wrestling with questions of guilt, not of love. You know, he sounded like he wanted to shoulder the guilt of the whole rotten world! Why should a man like Jacob feel that way? I don't understand!"

"You will. Jacob never stopped believing in God . . . in a God who *cared*, and he called Him the caring God. But because he had seen what happened to the Jews in Lodz, and not only by the Nazis, he began to have doubts about his all-caring God. I think he felt that God wasn't giving enough of a chance to His people. He brooded about that, Mottele. I think he was

ashamed, as a yeshiva man, of his doubts, and he felt guilty
about them. If it helps you, Mottele, I know that Jacob always
felt a bit relieved when Misha assigned him to dangerous missions . . . like this last one."

"He did, Jenya?"

"Because then he was forced to focus, he told me, on an act
of retribution. It gave him real direction, a sense of purpose
again. He didn't have to—what did you say?—shoulder the
world's guilt for a while. He didn't have to"—she tried a small
joke—"*dray* his *kopf* for a change."

Mottele looked at her, and he smiled, too.

"That's what he meant, then, when he said that the shadow
of Cain had fallen over the image of God?"

"I think so, yes."

The two friends fell silent. The bunker was cold and damp,
and they stayed in their coats, brooding, each of them thankful
for the other's presence. Jenya got up to light a candle. She let
the wick dribble grease on the table, which was made from an
empty cable wheel, then she stood the candle in the grease, and
its light threw strange shadow figures on the wall. Mottele,
watching the reflections, remembered how he and his sister,
Batya, would manipulate their fingers to turn them into rabbits
and geese; when he made a goose he would honk, and Batya
would laugh.

"Jacob did a strange thing before you came in with our lunch
that day," Mottele said, staring at the shadows. "He made a joke
about . . . about little kids. Then he put his head down and he
cried."

"So . . . Jacob did that?"

"I told him to stop, Jenya. Then you came with our lunch."

"What do you think made him cry, Mottele?"

"I don't know. It was just—well, he made a joke about me
being in love with Mirel. Mirel! Then he put his head down on
the table and cried."

Jenya, understanding, caught her breath sharply. "That's another reason why I wanted you to come, Mottele. You know that
map Jacob drew, showing where he'd left his son? He always
kept it on him, and now . . ."

"It's all right, Jenya. He made two copies, and asked me to hold on to one, keep it with my violin."

"Oh, thank God."

"The map's in my bunker with my violin. I'll go and get it, Jenya."

"No, not yet, Mottele!" Jenya's voice was suddenly urgent, worried.

"But I'll come right back. And I'll bring some coffee."

"Don't go, Mottele!"

"I'll come back."

"No, no! Stay with me. Just a bit longer."

"But wouldn't you like coffee, too?"

"Please!"

"Well, all right, Jenya."

So they continued to sit together, until the candle burned itself into the thickly spreading grease, and Jenya rose to light another. A sense of foreboding had descended on Mottele. He felt that Jenya was frightened, and she shouldn't be so frightened. He didn't know what to do. And why wasn't Sarah here to comfort her friend?

He longed to see Sarah himself.

As with Jacob, he couldn't bring himself to talk about his feelings for Sarah with Jenya, either.

At last he burst out, "I'm hungry, Jenya!"

"All right, little brother," she said, and managed a small laugh. "Go and eat, then. There'll be food in the radio hut, and coffee. Bring me back some coffee."

"And the map?"

"Yes, yes, the map."

"Would you like Sarah to come, too?"

"She'll be here soon, Mottele."

He opened the door and maneuvered his way up the few steps that had been hacked out of the ice. It was getting dark, and the snow had started again, powdering the ice and fogging the trees. The steadily falling flakes seemed to spread a hush over the campsite. The tall oaks and beeches, opaque in the whiteness, marched toward the horizon, becoming faint until they faded out. Mottele tried to will himself, on his way to the

bunker, to stop thinking about Jacob lying out there, somewhere beyond the edge. But it was no use.

He was still trying to shove the image of his dead friend to the
back of his mind, when he saw snow-shrouded figures—those of
Lyonka and Sarah—coming out of his bunker. Their coats hung
over their shoulders. He saw them start to go in the opposite
direction, toward the communications hut, when they stopped.
They seemed to be oblivious to everything but themselves.

He watched Lyonka pull Sarah to him, and hold her tightly.
They kissed for a long time, Sarah pressing against her lover;
and when her coat fell from her shoulders, it lay in a heap,
unheeded by them.

Mottele wanted to run away, to hide. He thought he would
burst with the strange mixture of fury and despair that pounded
his head, but he was too fascinated to stop watching. After a
while, Lyonka picked up Sarah's coat and hung it back on her
shoulders. Then, with their arms around each other, they went
on, stepping carefully, sliding, holding each other close, to the
radio hut. The boy stared after them. He found that he was
trembling.

"Fool, you'll freeze to death here!" he scolded, but it was as
though another Mottele, standing outside his skin, was speaking. Then he got himself to move into the shelter, and he fum-
bled for a match to light the candle stub.

Lyonka's cot, in wild disarray, told its own story, and after a
glance, Mottele avoided looking at it. The shadowy figures flick-
ering on the wall, no longer brought back nostalgic memories,
but looked sinister to him. He wanted to get back to Jenya
quickly.

The boy went to his cot and opened his violin case. He was
thankful he hadn't left it in its usual corner in the radio hut.
When word had come of Jacob's death he had carried the violin
back to their quarters. The violin was family, and though it
might suffer from the cold in the bunker, Mottele wanted it
with him. Now, from under the green felt lining in the case, he
pulled out the sheet of ruled copybook paper on which Jacob
and Lyonka had drawn the map.

Mottele looked at it dully. He studied the lines and place

names, and wondered what the Gentile family, in that eastern
Polish village, was like, and if they had cared for the infant
properly. He tried to remember the baby's name, but he
couldn't.

"You can't remember anything!" he scolded, and it seemed
again to be the other Mottele speaking.

He stuck the map in his pocket, blew out the light and started
back to Jenya. She was still sitting, as though immobilized, but
she looked up gratefully when the boy came in. He was tense
and sad-eyed, and only then remembered that he hadn't
brought the coffee.

"I'm sorry, Jenya—I forgot the coffee."

"Never mind. Let me see the map, Mottele, and we can go
to the communications hut together."

"No!"

"No?" She studied the boy's face.

"Maybe . . . later."

Jenya took the map, then put it down, and she asked very
gently, "Tell me, Mottele, has something upset you?"

"It's nothing."

"You can tell me, Mottele. Don't be afraid."

"I don't want to talk about it."

"But I made you talk about Jacob. You should . . ."

"There's nothing to talk about."

"Then let me guess, Mottele." Jenya went on quietly, respect-
ing the boy's sensitivity. "Does it have to do with Sarah and
Lyonka? Did you see them?" The boy twisted away. "Sarah's
not here because I told her to go to Lyonka and be with him.
She was so thankful that Lyonka was spared."

Mottele said nothing.

"They love each other, Mottele."

The boy sat quite still. Jenya went on, fearing to hurt him,
fearing his resentment. "Try to understand, Mottele. It's wonderful that Sarah is able to feel good again, to *give* love to
someone again. She was badly hurt and she's been so ill. It's
wonderful to feel the power to give love, Mottele. I know, and
now Sarah knows."

"Why are you going on?"

"Be happy for her, Mottele."

"Let's change the subject!"

"All right."

The boy sat very upright, with his hands clasped in front of him, his mouth a tight line of control.

"Mottele . . . ?"

"What is it now, Jenya?"

"Mottele, Jacob was my man, a very big man, you know. But you remember—when he needed to, he let himself cry."

The boy wept then. His head went down, and he let himself cry for Jacob, and for Jenya, and for himself. And the Mottele who stood outside his skin watched him weeping and didn't scold him this time and Jenya took him in her arms.

After a bit, the old Jenya took charge.

"Now dry your eyes. Come on, we're going to the hut and get some food in us and hot coffee. I've decided I'm very hungry, Mottele. Nu?"

The boy looked up and he grinned. He rose and straightened his uniform and told her he was hungry, too. As they walked toward the hut, he said, "There's something I can't remember, Jenya. The name of Jacob's son."

The girl's eyes clouded as she took Mottele's arm. "It's Ephraim. In the Bible, it's written that God said, 'How shall I give thee up, Ephraim?' He was Joseph's younger son."

Mottele was fascinated. "Those were Jacob's words, too!"

"And now they're mine, Mottele," said Jenya.

*Yea, though I walk through the valley
of the shadow of death . . .*

PSALM 23:4

17

Warsaw is not Lodz, Jacob had said. . . .

At about the time that Jacob fell in battle, another man like
Jacob was rising to battle the enemy not far from the forest
fighters, in a ghetto youth movement in the Warsaw ghetto.
The news of that ghetto uprising, which was to shake up the
whole world at last, came to Mottele over the radio in bits and
pieces. Ivan was now helping on translations and he and Mottele were carrying the reports in the camp paper. They heard
that the Polish underground, outside the Warsaw ghetto wall,
had managed to smuggle a few revolvers and grenades to
ghetto activists; not much of an arsenal for attacking enemy
armor, the ghetto radioed, but as usual the Jews had a wry
Yiddish saying for that: "Even when there's no luck, there has
to be some luck!"

Vengeance—they'll have their vengeance now, Jacob! Mottele thought as he copied down the communiqués, and the boy
hoped that wasn't mere wishful thinking. Everyone knew what
the activists inside Europe's biggest ghetto could expect from
the Germans. Heinrich Himmler, the SS chief, visiting the
ghetto that January, had been chagrined to find that sixty thousand Jews still existed within it, the remainder of the half million who had been there. He personally ordered them
"removed" at once.

But another young Mordechai—Mordechai Anielewicz of
Warsaw—had decided differently. At twenty-three, a Zionist
militant, this Mordechai commanded the ghetto's Jewish Com-

bat Organization, known in the ghetto by its initials, ZOB. No mystic like Jacob, Mordechai Anielewicz had steeped himself in political and premilitary training since he was twelve. A slender man of medium height, wiry and intense, the ZOB commander was more interested in Zionist literature than the Bible. At first he and his followers had focused on material means—funds with which to get guns and ammunition, there still being a few relatively rich Jews in the ghetto who had managed to buy off their own deportations; and some small arms which a few Polish Socialist patriots outside the wall managed to smuggle in.

In late January of 1943, the SS began an *Aktion* with orders to kill any resisters and deport all the other Jews from the ghetto. They were ordered to inflict damage and set fire to blocks of houses, roasting both combatants and noncombatants, to wipe out the area. It was the Germans with tanks, explosives, machine guns and rifles against the Jews with revolvers, homemade weapons, a few grenades, sandbags and furniture. Commander Anielewicz gave the order: "Don't go to your death without a fight! Stand up for yourselves! Get hold of an ax, an iron bar, a knife . . . !" The one advantage the Warsaw militants retained was the element of surprise: the Germans never expected to be met with a rain of bullets!

Fighting had spread to nearby streets, with the biggest battle near Niska Street, headed by the young Jewish commander himself, and the activists fired on the SS, who were herding some Jews before them, taking the Germans by complete surprise. As the poet Yitzhak Katzenelson, fighting with the underground, was to write of the German reaction to this amazing episode:

> They did not know, they did not believe.
> The Jews are shooting!
> I heard an ugly voice in a corrupt mouth,
>   before he breathed his last unclean breath,
> Not his normal shout I heard,
> Only a horrified cry: "Is it possible?"

The courage of the Warsaw Jews certainly heartened the Polish non-Jews outside the wall—they relayed respectful reports to Allied and partisan listeners. After four days, the Germans lifted that particular siege of the Warsaw ghetto.

"Obviously, it couldn't have been because of our military strength," the ghetto underground radio reported dryly. "The Germans apparently fear that the revolt may spread to the Aryan side of Warsaw, outside the wall. Also, the Germans need all the transportation they can get for their troops retreating from Stalingrad."

Misha studied every communiqué of the uprising with a mixture of admiration and apprehension. He knew what the outcome had to be, unless the Allies would help by bombing the ghetto, and thus freeing the Jews.

"The Nazi bastards are losing the war," Misha told Mottele. "They're retreating, and their blitzkrieg against Stalingrad has failed. But they're still obsessed with their 'Jewish War.' Those Warsaw partisans have incredible guts! What we'd give to have Jacob know about this—eh, Mottele?"

He saw the boy stiffen at the mention of Jacob.

"Death is also part of life," Misha went on in a measured tone. "This Mordechai of Warsaw and his partisans know the price they may have to pay. They're ready to pay it; it's the only real part of their life now."

"To have their vengeance, like us," Mottele murmured.

"Correct. When you write this up for the paper, lad, be sure to make the contrast with Lodz ghetto. Jacob would have liked that, don't you think?"

All through that January and February and March, the Warsaw ghetto drama held partisan, if not world, attention. Small companies of Commander Anielewicz's ZOB regularly manned positions inside the wall—in the "central ghetto," the "brushmakers' ghetto," the "workshops ghetto"; at night they made bombs, mines and Molotov cocktails, dug bunkers and built hiding places in attics and stairwells. They hoped that their struggle would spill over the wall to the Polish population, also under the German heel, and rally it to their defense. If that could happen, who could tell what might follow in the outside world?

SS Chief Himmler was infuriated by this unseemly tumult and the German setback. He issued an order which said, "The events in Warsaw prove how dangerous these Jews are." Therefore the ghetto now had to be attacked "with all severity and with merciless harshness." His new plan was to give the Führer a big present on April 19—Hitler's fifty-fourth birthday: a *Judenrein* Warsaw, a Warsaw "clean of Jews" within three days.

In fact, the revolt by the Warsaw partisans took four weeks, and before it came to a fiery end, the final uprising and slaughter were to write one of the most bloody and heroic chapters in Holocaust history. The world at war looked on with, at the least, fascination.

The night before the big SS *Aktion* was Passover. Commander Anielewicz met secretly with his leaders in a bunker at 18 Mila Street, and distributed weapons, ammunition and food. He gave orders to barricade entrances to all streets and houses, using furniture, sandbags, whatever they could find, and assigned patrols. Except for the patrols, not a Jew was on the street that first Seder night. While the Jews "celebrated" without matzohs, chanting the prayers they knew by heart, which told of deliverance from Egyptian bondage, powerful German contingents took up positions with machine guns on the wall, and manned roads outside the ghetto to cut off escape.

Himmler had ordered a dedicated Nazi, SS General Jürgen Stroop, to supervise the liquidation of the ghetto, and Stroop, a forty-eight-year-old veteran of campaigns in Poland and Russia, had at his disposal an armored battalion, a cavalry battalion, German police battalions, Ukrainian and Polish police squads, Latvian and Lithuanian police units, artillery, engineers and a demolition squad—in all, some two thousand heavily armed men, and a reserve force of seven thousand. Against that armada, the Jews had about a thousand young men and women, who were armed with a few hundred revolvers, rifles and grenades, and their sandbags and furniture.

Over the border, the forest fighters could only look on anxiously. The partisans came and went in the radio hut, from which Mottele and Ivan hardly moved. The two friends wrote down the date of Himmler's promised "birthday present" to Hitler, and the fact that this was Passover, with the Warsaw Jews still holding out. "The waiting is horrible," Mottele wrote, saying the words out loud to Ivan, "but it's not like what Jacob told us about Lodz!"

The shocked world gave international publicity to the "coming event," which irritated Himmler and his generals, but *words* were all that the world sent to the ghetto. The small arsenal began to give out, and the Germans started to burn the ghetto down. Some pockets of resistance managed still to hold out and set fire to tanks; and a Polish group outside the wall smuggled in more arms, then joined their Jewish comrades in battle inside the wall.

But with weapons gone, and the ghetto in flames, the struggle was doomed. Commander Anielewicz had managed to get a letter to his deputy on the "Aryan" side of Warsaw who was trying to get more arms—and Mottele, who was now living in the radio hut, feverishly recorded it when it was broadcast:

It is quite clear to us what happened has by far surpassed all our expectations. . . . Now, however, our strength is weakening and dwindling. We stand at the brink of the abyss. . . . I am not able to describe to you the conditions in which the Jews in the ghetto "live" now. . . . Their fate is sealed, though they are still trying to hide in all kinds of places. It is impossible to light a candle because of the lack of air. . . . Greetings to you:

We bid you farewell, you on the "outside." Perhaps a miracle will happen, and we will see each other one day. Still, I doubt it. I doubt it very much. . . . The last wish of my life has come true. Jewish self-defense has become reality. Jewish resistance and vengeance have been transformed into acts. I am happy to have found myself among the first fighting Jews in the ghetto.

When combatants finally took to the sewers in an attempt to get to the "Aryan" side outside the wall, German engineers flooded the sewers, exploded smoke and chemical bombs inside them, and cut off escape. About a hundred partisans were left in the headquarters bunker at 18 Mila Street. Germans stationed themselves outside and demanded that they surrender. When they received a "no surrender," the Germans brought up heavy guns, and began to dynamite the bunker. And those inside—like their historic counterparts defending Masada against the Romans—chose to die at their own hands. One of them was the young commander Mordechai Anielewicz.

The revolt broken, the Germans tore down the blue-and-white Jewish flag with its Star of David, and the white-and-red Polish flag, and burned them. And the SS began to photograph and feast its eyes on the last of the Jews jumping from blazing rooftops and balconies, dashing themselves to bits on the ground below. Many of them were living torches before they reached the ground. The pictures of that spectacle were to be part of the birthday present. The Wehrmacht and the SS finished off the ghetto; those Jews not massacred in the uprising were sent to the killing centers of Maidanek and Treblinka.

On May 16, General Stroop was pleased to report to Himmler that Hitler's birthday present was all wrapped up: "The former Jewish quarter no longer exists. An explosion (for which the Jews, themselves, were responsible) destroyed the Warsaw synagogue. The *Grossaktion* is terminated."

Across the Polish-Russian border, Misha and his partisans got the terrible news at the same time that, ironically, Joseph Goebbels, propaganda minister, was recording the immense damage to German cities and industries by Allied bombs: "The day raids by American bombers are creating extraordinary difficulties. At Kiel . . . very serious damage to military and technical installations of the Navy . . . If this continues we shall have to face serious consequences which in the long run will prove unbearable. . . ."

The Germans were losing the war against superior armies on all fronts, and the tables were being turned on them in that savage spring of 1943: they had been forced to withdraw all submarines from the North Atlantic, as the Allies kept sinking their U-boats; and the Russians had won the major battles on the

Eastern front. But still the Nazis could boast about the success of their "Jewish War"—their feats against the *Untermenschen,* the subhumans, and their victory over the Warsaw ghetto.

"Yes, they can brag about that," Misha told Mottele in a hard tone. "They don't have much else on their plate right now, do they? They can hand that birthday present to Hitler."

"Well, that's quite a present," Mottele said glumly.

"Stop your moping, lad!" Misha retorted. "The Warsaw partisans chose to defend their honor—they *chose* the way they died! Don't forget they took plenty of Germans with them. And they shook up not only the Nazis but the world!"

"That's the way we're to see it, Diadia Misha?"

"It's what happened!"

"And that's the way I should write it up?"

"Of course! Write it plain, my son! And dedicate the issue of the newspaper to Jacob of Lodz!"

*Haman sought to destroy all the Jews
that were throughout the whole kingdom
of Ahasuerus, even the people of Mordechai.*

ESTHER 3:6

18

The weather was growing milder, and the whole camp had come out of the bunkers and tunnels to enjoy it, relishing the bright sun which was melting snow and ice. The partisans' great friend, the forest, was slushy and growing green again. The howls of the wolves were fading every day now, as the "time of the singing of birds . . . the voice of the turtle" came back to the land. And with it, good tidings that the fortunes of war were definitely changing in the Allies' favor. In the context of these sweeping historic changes, the partisan movement became more crucial.

No longer were Misha's partisans and the scores of smaller detachments to operate as "free" units: Moscow commanded them to coordinate their strategy—for all were now to come under the umbrella control of the High Command. By spring of 1943, about twenty thousand Jewish fighters were in partisan units—some units were all Jewish, some mixed—and the Jews had the hardest choice to make: whether to fight in the ghetto or face an unpredictable fate in the forest. But with the tides of Nazi occupation ebbing, a whole new phase of partisan warfare was taking on dramatic scope: throughout Russia, tens of thousands of ordinary citizens left the cities and villages to join the forest partisans, to create what became virtually a "Soviet Republic of Partisans" in the heart of the occupied areas. Ties with the Red Army command were powerfully strengthened, the aim being to provoke a mass national resistance movement to drive the Nazis out. So important had the partisan movement

become that commanders of the larger units were now sum-
moned to Moscow for military conferences.

Moscow was well aware that in certain places the Russian
populace had welcomed the invaders as "liberators," col-
laborating with the enemy by handing over or slaughtering
partisans, especially Jewish partisans. But there were many
more now who supported the partisans; indeed, without their
support, the partisan/guerrilla war might never have expanded
at all. They were to prove that Hitler and his Wehrmacht had
made a major mistake by not taking the partisan movement
seriously enough from the beginning. The German generals,
those not consulting astrologers on mountaintops, now took
note of large sections of the Russian people voluntarily going
into the forests with their goods, turning the scattered partisan
units into this astonishing mass people's movement.

By the time of this mass movement, the Jewish fighters were
at least being credited with exceptional qualities of survival.
What Moscow failed to understand, or chose not to, was that the
Jews cherished their own units for psychological as well as military reasons. By their example, they were motivating other
Jews to escape to their side; they inspired ambition that their
combat operations would, historically, be credited to Jews. In
this they were wrong, and one thing they wryly came to realize
was *never:* never would the Soviet High Command credit their
guerrilla actions to them as *Jews.* Though Hitler had made war
on the Jews, they were not allowed to fight as Jews, but as
operatives "on the soil" of the Ukraine, Byelorussia, Poland,
Lithuania, Estonia, etc. The Russians, from the High Command
down to the lowly peasant, refused to concede the psychological imperative in all this for the Jewish partisans.

Or could it be, Misha sometimes reflected caustically, that the
living presence of the Jews among them was a living reminder
of guilt—collective guilt? World guilt? Too great a responsibility
for the Russians and the rest of the Allies to bear?

Diadia Misha had got direct instructions from the High Command—to take into his unit a large group of Ukrainian youths.

The order came from the great Marshal Kliment Voroshilov himself. The marshal also radioed warm congratulations to Misha on his unit's daring military exploits, and announced that Misha had been awarded the rank of captain. Finally, the marshal said he wanted to offer him a civil engineering job away from the front.

Diadia Misha was pleased, but not unduly impressed. The bespectacled businessman-engineer cum soldier promptly instructed his wireless operator to radio back to the marshal his thanks and his plain objective: "My aim is to pursue our vengeance campaign and reach Berlin as victor and as Jew. I will redeem my last debt from Hitler in Berlin."

The Ukrainian youths dashing into Misha's camp brought the reason for their transfer: a German military company was reconnoitering the forests, between the towns of Zhitomir and Kiev, with orders to destroy partisans; its infantry stretched over twenty kilometers and was moving with a tank force through the forest, with Messerschmitt planes to give them cover, shooting the civilian population down indiscriminately— a farmer working in his field, a woman collecting mushrooms, a boy minding the cows. Misha radioed to Moscow for instructions. He was ordered to mine the roads, first, where the Germans were advancing; if he found that his partisans were seriously outnumbered, they were to shift camp, but to keep the High Command informed.

The roads were mined. But Misha worried about the strength of a tank force and Messerschmitts, and their obvious strategy —to push the partisans into the River Uzh nearby. Partisan units in the general area were alerted, and from his scouts Misha estimated that the Germans were too close and too numerous for comfort. He sent a patrol to the river, to find the shallowest reedy place, safe from the roads where the German punitive force was moving, and to build a serviceable bridge of tree trunks across the shallows. Misha was not a little morose. The brigade's camp had been the best equipped that his men had known in all their forest wanderings, a real home for many months; he hated to leave it for another, unknown part of the forest.

But he didn't hesitate. As soon as the bridge was ready, he gave the order to move en masse to the River Uzh. There, as Captain Misha of his mixed brigade, he stood on shore, making certain that the partisans could navigate their way over the fragile bridge; he watched the family-camp members gingerly start over, the new Ukrainian youths eagerly helping the old ones and the infants and carrying food, medicines and surplus weapons. They were taking little enough with them, for, to ease the movement of camp, Misha had ordered the rest of the supplies and the carts destroyed. With civilians safely across, Misha went to stand on the opposite shore to await the partisans' rear contingent.

They had strapped on their ammunition, and they held their rifles at the ready, looking around them as they came across. Ivan was moving very slowly. He was just behind Mottele and dragging his bad leg, muttering oaths about the weight of the wireless strapped to his shoulder. The partisans were nearly across the river when two Messerschmitts darted over their heads. The planes began to shower the area with bullets. Most of the partisans had time to run the rest of the way, but a few jumped into the river and had to swim for it. Ivan was among the latter. He held the wireless over his head, as he struggled to paddle his way across, but he dropped the small leather bag that contained the batteries and, to his horror, watched it sink. Mottele and two partisans jumped into the river to help Ivan, who was cursing wildly. The bullets by now were raining down like devouring birds, but the three of them managed to keep Ivan afloat and get to the other side.

Threatening them all from a distance were several tanks, and still circling above them the planes. Misha reckoned that enemy infantry would probably arrive in a short time, and he wanted to alert the Russian High Command to send help—not only for them but for other partisan units converging at the river. When darkness came, he intended to get his group as far into the forest as he could until help arrived.

There was one serious problem.

"We can't use the goddamn wireless!" Ivan wailed. "The batteries are at the bottom of the river! I dropped the bag when

I fell in, and it's probably drifted off."

"Well, if you aren't the prize *shlamazel!*" Mottele scolded, as he went to help his friend unstrap the wireless from his shoulder.

"What's that mean, Mottele?"

"Damn unlucky, that's what it means!"

"That's enough, Mottele," said Misha worriedly. "We've got a problem, and not much time."

He called his brigade commanders together.

Everyone was bone weary and too tense to believe their luck would hold, with the Germans so close. Several bullets had already found their mark, and Sarah and Jenya were giving what first aid they could. The commanders had to admit they were frustrated; they couldn't offer a solution to the problem of the drowned batteries. They recommended that the partisans should give up the radio and get moving at once, hoping for the best.

Mottele had been listening to the consultation. Now he stared at the river, and interrupted the men.

"Misha, I can swim to the spot where Ivan dropped the bag," he said, "and bring it back myself."

"That's impossible, lad," Misha said brusquely. "The Germans will notice you at once."

"They won't see me, Uncle Misha," Mottele insisted. "I'll be swimming under the water, there and back."

"Now, how can you be such a long time under the water? It's impossible; out of the question. The planes are out in force, and their tanks are on the other shore. You could endanger all of us, Mottele."

"You don't understand! I can stay under the water for hours, if I need to," Mottele continued stubbornly.

"Oh, rubbish!"

"But I can, Misha!"

"You're making me very angry with such rubbish!"

"No, Papa, it's not rubbish," Lyonka put in. "I've seen Mottele do this, when we've been fishing. It's amazing. But I really think he can pull it off safely, without alerting the Germans. I say let Mottele give it a try."

Misha looked from Mottele to his son with disbelief. Quickly, the boy stripped off his clothes and boots; then he crawled to the shore. He pulled up several tall reeds growing in the water, put one into his mouth, held the remaining reeds for replacements, and slowly let himself into the water. Mottele went down, down, and almost immediately the upper end of the reed could be seen moving slowly toward the spot where Ivan had fallen off the bridge.

The partisans, watching the enemy's position across the river through binoculars, could see the Germans looking intently in their direction; the enemy seemed to be listening for every move and whisper. In his heart, Misha mocked the enemy concentration, completely unaware of a Jewish boy on a dangerous mission under that slim tube floating on the river. But he and every partisan held their breath, following the reed as it circled the crucial spot, then stopped. Soon it started back to the partisans, and a few minutes after, Mottele was with them again. Victoriously, he handed the little leather bag to Misha.

Late that night, in the denser protection of the forest, after his small, tired little army and the civilians had lain down for a few hours' sleep, Misha added a note to his daily diary: "After we had hurriedly withdrawn to the forest, far away from the river, Moscow could receive my SOS—thanks to our Mottele."

. . . for love is strong as death
Jealousy is cruel as the grave . . .

SONG OF SONGS 8:6

19

"That was some stunt, Mottele."

"It was nothing."

"*I* was very impressed."

"Just trick swimming. Anyone can learn it, Sarah."

"Where did *you* learn it?"

"You forget I was a farm boy. My village had a sawmill. I used to watch the logs coming downriver, and sometimes I would ride them."

"Ride them?"

"Well, you have fun running on them, diving off, swimming around the logs in all kinds of situations. I liked staying under water. I got good at it. I could play with the fish deep down."

"You certainly went deep down to save that leather bag with the batteries. And the whole situation."

"Come on, Sarah! So we'd have made contact with another partisan unit and used their wireless."

"Don't brush it off, Mottele. You were good! Misha says you bought time for us. He says you ought to get a medal!"

"Oh, sure."

"Wouldn't you like a medal, little brother?"

"Sarah, don't be so silly!"

"Well, wouldn't you?"

"A real kibitzer!"

"You wouldn't deprive us of a chance to celebrate, get us all dancing again!"

"So celebrate!"

"There has to be an event, a reason."

"Well, not this."

"Don't be shy, Mottele. You're a big hero!"

"A hero yet! *Gevalt!*"

"Mottele, come here!"

"No . . . don't!"

"Why not?"

"I just don't like to be touched!"

"Since when?"

"Since when? Since always."

"That's not true."

"I don't like it."

"It's since Jacob died, isn't it?"

"No."

"Since Jacob died—say it, Mottele!"

"No."

"Mottele, it's me, isn't it? *Look* at me, love!"

"All right, I'm looking. So?"

"Stop your running, Mottele. I don't like it, little brother."

"And I don't like you little-brothering me!"

"All right. But listen to me, Mottele. No, don't turn away again! You listen! Mottele, I have to tell you something, share this with you. *Please . . . !*

"What, Sarah?"

"Well, it's just . . . I don't know how to tell you. . . . Look at me, Mottele, help me! I want to share it with you!"

"All right, then."

"Well, it's just . . . Mottele, I love Lyonka, yes, but I love you, Mottele, too. Can you understand me? In some ways, I think I love you *more* than Lyonka. Because you're Mottele, and you're my family. You're my little brother who was killed in Korets. Now do you understand? Now, you see, I can say all of it straight out."

"All right, you've said it, Sarah."

"Listen, I don't know what you saw or what you must think. . . . Jenya told me."

"Nothing to talk about."

"No! It was beautiful, Mottele! It's so hard to explain, but I want you to be happy for me, too. It's wonderful to feel, inside, deep inside, the . . . power to give love to someone. I feel that, and one day you'll understand, little brother."

"It's all right, Sarah."

"No, I don't feel it's all right yet."

"Well, it will be."

"Oh, I want it to be, Mottele. I need you, and that's it in a nutshell! Oh, Mottele, I seem to have a real family again. I seem to feel . . . Do you know what season of the year this is, Mottele?"

"Season?"

"Yes, season. It's just been Passover."

"In this crazy place, too."

"But we weren't able to celebrate, have a Seder or the matzohs, nothing. And since the Warsaw action, I've been thinking what it was like in Korets at Passover time . . . in your village, too, Mottele?"

"I remember."

"You know, I've been dreaming about it, and it's so real, so true. I see Mama washing down all the doors and windows, preparing for *Yontiff.* She has to scrub everything perfect, and I'm helping her. It takes Mama over a week to bake the matzohs. The two of us knit new woolen dresses for ourselves, rose-colored for her, pale pink for me, with scallops at the necks and hems; and blue sweaters for Papa and my little brother. They order new suits from the tailor, of course, but the tailor forgets to put pockets in my brother's suit and he's angry. The Seder table is laid—it shines with all our silver and crystal—shining silver candelabra on the white lace tablecloth. We use the best dishes, the long-stemmed wineglasses. Everything on the table shines like all the faces around the table. Mama hides the three matzohs in their special holder near Papa's place. . . ."

"Papa makes the *Kiddush.* . . ."

"Papa fills the glasses from the bottle of red wine. What a treat, Mottele."

"In front of Papa is the Seder plate with the Passover symbols—Mama has roasted the shank bone, it's on the silver plate with the chopped apple and lettuce and bitter herbs and parsley. . . ."

"Papa starts reading from the Haggadah. . . ."

" 'Blessed art Thou, O Eternal, our God . . .' "

"Go on, Mottele!"

" '. . . King of the Universe, Creator of the fruit of the vine!' "

"Papa begins the story of remembrance—how Pharaoh enslaved the Jewish people in Egypt, and God sent down the ten plagues until Pharaoh was so frightened he begged the Jews to leave Egypt. . . ."

" 'Slaves we were . . . *Avodim hoyeenu . . .*' "

"Yes, yes, Mottele . . . and my brother gets up—he's feeling very important—he's the son of the house and he has to ask the traditional four questions of Papa. . . ."

" 'Wherefore is this night distinguished from all other nights?' Why do we have only matzohs tonight, when we can eat matzohs all the year round—why only bitter herbs—why dip the egg in salt water twice—why recline at the table tonight?"

"Yes, and Papa gives the answers. . . ."

"How Moses led the Jews away from Pharaoh and out of bondage in Egypt, but Pharaoh changed his mind and sent his army after the Jews. But when we reached the Red Sea, Moses stretched forth his rod. . . ."

"Show me, Mottele, the way Papa . . ."

". . . and split the sea like this! And then the Jews passed safely to the other side. But not the Egyptians! The sea closed over them and their chariots, and the sea drowned all of them."

"And after that the Jews spent forty years wandering in the wilderness, and Moses received the Law on Mount Sinai, and we wandered until God brought us to the Land of Israel."

"And by this time, we're all starving! But now we can eat, Sarah. What a supper Mama's got before us! Gefilte fish, and chicken soup with matzoh balls, and a tzimmes of carrots, bottles of orange soda, her big, *Pesadik,* beautiful sponge cake. . . ."

"My mouth's watering, Mottele!"

"I can remember every detail."

"A banquet. But what about-Elijah!"

"Yes, Elijah. Papa fills an extra glass of wine to the brim for the 'special guest,' and I have to go to the door to let him in— Elijah, the Prophet. It's my duty to go and let him in, so he can tell us of the final redemption, but I'm scared, Sarah. I was always scared of that moment when I had to let Elijah in. I can never figure out how Elijah can get in the door of every Jew in the world at the same time. I imagine that every door is opening when I open ours, but . . . but our house is chosen, and he's coming in, but we can't see him!"

"I'm allowed to go to the door with my brother."

"Was he scared, too, Sarah?"

"We were both scared!"

"After we're full up with all the food, we sing . . ."

". . . the old Seder songs. *Chad Gad-Yoh?*"

"The big one."

"Can you sing it, Mottele?"

" 'One kid, one kid—that Father bought
for two zuzim—one kid, one kid.
Along came the cat, and ate the kid that
Father bought for two zuzim—one kid, one kid.
Along came the dog, and bit the cat that ate
the kid that Father bought for two zuzim—one kid, one kid.
Along came the stick and beat the dog that bit
the cat that ate the kid that Father bought
for two zuzim—one kid, one kid. . . .' "

"The children's song, so simple, so old . . ."

"So true for today, Sarah."

"You mean the way people are beating up others, gobbling up one another!"

"I learned it in *cheder.*"

"It seems like yesterday, Mottele."

"To me, too, Sarah."

"Papa and Mama were king and queen at Seder."

"In our house, too."

"We were allowed to drink lots of wine. We all felt drowsy, warm, safe. We fell asleep right after it was over, Mottele."

"In our house, too."

"It's like yesterday."

"Very close, Sarah."

"Thank you, thank you, little brother."

"What for?"

"For making such a beautiful Seder for me!"

"I enjoyed it, too, Sarah."

"It was very nice, very real!"

"To me, too."

"Will you give me a kiss for *Yontiff*, little brother?"

"All right."

"Thank you. *Gut Yontiff*, Mottele."

"Gut Yontiff, Sarah."

With the Moscow High Command now insisting that Jews could no longer maintain themselves in separate and "free" fighting Jewish units, the Jewish partisans were forced, for the most part, to bow to that authority. Such Jews who would not integrate into the "territorial" units were simply freed as individuals, left to fend for themselves in the forests. Integrate or be damned, was the word from the High Command.

Diadia Misha had voluntarily integrated, and by 1943, his brigade of several hundreds had only 40 percent Jewish partisans. Misha rationalized that it was good enough that a Jew—himself—headed a brigade of White Russians, Ukrainians *and* Jews; that his family camp, nearly all Jewish, remained intact; that everyone under his command knew he would tolerate no nonsense. But since Jacob's death, Misha had to admit to himself he was feeling his Jewish losses deeply. Every person in his camp meant a life saved from the enemy—but he knew it was the Jewish lives that mattered most to him.

From the beginning of this odyssey, Misha had felt the Jewish losses were the hardest to take: there would be few enough Jews left at the end of this terrible war—for already close to three million Jews in Poland alone, mainly the defenseless, women and children, the elderly and the sick, had been murdered.

Little wonder, Misha reflected, that Jacob had driven himself nearly insane with his doubts about humanity and about God. You'd have to be God Himself, Misha thought bitterly, to wrestle with the whys and wherefores of the Highest Command of all. So, as Jacob finally had managed to do, Misha left God out of it; he concentrated on the living and on taking vengeance. Anyway, he quipped inwardly, that attitude should admirably suit the angry Old Testament Old Boy—if there was one!

But with all the amateur strategy that was succeeding against a disciplined, well-equipped enemy, Misha never really got used to his soldiering. He often longed for the time when he could be alone again with a few men who knew nothing but music, and the chorales. Or with a drawing board, devising a new piece of machinery for a factory. Or with his books. But he quickly gave such thoughts the back of his hand: he was quite grateful to God—at such times he believed in God and Fate—that Symcha, his son, had been spared to him; that his son and Sarah were at last getting something out of this strange odyssey; that Mottele was with him.

The past year had wrought a radical change in Misha's appearance. His eyebrows had gone white with the rest of his thinning hair. His once-benign brown eyes were now deep-set and coldly appraising behind the steel-rimmed spectacles. The lined face retained the old baggy look, but the jaw stuck forward like a ship's prow, and often Misha seemed so remote that even Lyonka could hardly glimpse behind the resolute, tough, outer man the papa he'd grown up with. All the external changes were easily apparent to those who'd been with Misha from the start; but inwardly, part of him would never change —the part that remained forever in Korets with his family and remembered friends, and the old, well-loved days.

The one person Misha could never be really tough with was Mottele. The boy in every way had come to mean the most precious human resource that Misha and his partisans had. He probably loved the boy, he secretly told himself, even more than he did Lyonka. Mottele was so damn intelligent and resourceful, so damn stubborn, with reason, not forgetting what a charmer he could also be when he wanted to. The lad's need for vengeance was, astonishingly, as mature as Misha's own. And where did he get such *chutzpah* from? That last stunt of his, underwater, under the noses of the Nazis, was incredible!

And so, when word came from Moscow that Misha's brigade was to assemble beyond the bridge spanning the River Pripet, there to join up with the Red Army's Kovpak Brigade in its advance against the Germans, Misha struggled with the problem of Mottele.

He did not want Mottele in that action. He felt Mottele would have to go, once and for all, with the family-camp civilians to the rear. Misha would tell the boy that they would surely meet again, somehow, at the end of the war. He, Captain Misha, would definitely arrange that with the Moscow High Command, and they would be reunited then and go on the long-awaited *aliyah* to Palestine. Misha built up the rosy future in his mind, but he did not underestimate what he was going to be up against with the boy.

Misha called his unit commanders together for the mission, which he told them would be the most dangerous of their forest careers.

"The Germans are in retreat," he said, "but they're digging in as they retreat, and they're returning fire with bloody accuracy, and they have air cover. The High Command has wirelessed all partisan groups in this area that it's vital to wage a diversionary action to enable the Russian brigade to fight back, cross the river, and be able to attack the Germans from both shores. Now comes the announcement we've been waiting for: If the joint action is successful, our partisans can expect to be joined permanently to the Red Army brigade coming over!"

Misha's partisans assembled outside headquarters, ready to march, fully armed and equipped for the action. A number of partisans were to remain behind, guarding the family camp, until the end of the action. Mottele, as Misha had expected, was the problem.

In his cut-down uniform and short polished boots, his automatic stuck in his belt, the boy stood boldly in the front row, his
fair hair blowing in the morning breeze, his eyes blazing furiously at Misha. In fact, he had taken his position alongside
Lyonka and Popov deliberately, expecting them to back him
up. Now he held himself as rigid as any soldier, fearing what he
knew was coming.

"Mottele, you are to stay behind with the family group, and
guard them with the other partisans. That's where I need you
today," Misha said bluntly.

The boy's face went white. He didn't speak or move. He
gripped his belt and maintained his rigid posture. But he could
not hold back the tears. He let them come, said nothing, and
continued to wait. The rest of the partisans stood silently.

"This is my firm decision," Misha went on rapidly, trying to
sound very military. "The Russian High Command has promised to move family-camp people to the rear after this mission.
I depend on you, lad, to take charge there. It's a very important
job, and in the rear you can also continue with your education."

"No!"

"After all, Mottele, you're only twelve!"

"I'm *not* a kid anymore!" Mottele burst out. "I'm thirteen
. . . nearly! I'm as much a partisan as . . . as anyone!"

"That you are, lad."

"Then I must go with you! I can be useful with this mission,
as a scout, or with the covering fire . . . just like I've been in the
forest. I'm very useful!"

Lyonka and Popov remained quite still, not taking their eyes
off Misha, fascinated and miserable. A heavy silence fell on the
gathering, for every man cherished their youngest partisan and
wanted his safety. Misha licked his dry lips, and tried to remain
firm.

"You're all of that, Mottele, but I'm under orders to do something about your future, about all the children of family camp!"

"I'm not family camp!" the boy rushed on violently. "I have
to stay with you, Misha! It's not just this mission. I'm an orphan
. . . and apart from you, Diadia Misha, and Lyonka, I have no

one in the world. I *won't* be separated from you. I *won't!*"

The men still looked straight ahead, tense and immobile, waiting to see how the furious exchange would come out.

"Well, Mottele, you've done it again," Misha said at last, with a short laugh. "Managed to pull out all the stops, haven't you? So who's trying to get rid of you?"

A great shout went up then from the gathering. One or two partisans yelled approval with relieved laughter. Lyonka grabbed the boy, and Mottele grinned up at Lyonka. Unashamedly, he wiped away his tears.

"All right, men, gather round," Captain Misha said. "Let's have a look at this map, and the work that's been cut out for us. It starts with this ambush here."

He held the map of the area, with the bridge and the River Pripet heavily marked, against a tree. Mottele went and stood close to Misha, as he briefed his partisans on the coming action.

20

Misha left a small contingent behind to guard the family camp, with Ivan as its group commander. He took the rest of his detachment, Mottele included, on the march to the River Pripet. They went by horse and on foot, with machine guns, rifles, automatics, grenades and supplies. Each one of the ragged little band moved with mixed emotions. This was the moment transcending all others—partisans recognized and fighting a joint action with the Red Army itself. The outcome could depend as much on their efforts as on those of the regulars. Misha's men had no idea of the size of the German units coming over; the partisans would have to move fast to get to the bridge ahead of them—a decent bridge this time, which would support their horses and equipment—and be waiting on the opposite shore like a "reception committee" for the Germans. It had to succeed!

They marched and rode all that day and night, bolstering themselves with an occasional pull on a brandy flask. They would have liked to show their feelings, whistle or sing as they went, but of course that could invite trouble; so they went quietly, envisaging the ambush, and later a marvelous meeting with the regulars, and who could tell—news from Moscow about relatives and friends?

They got to the river just as a cold, full moon broke in half and gradually faded out. A thick mist hung over the river, making a fine shield for the partisans as they lined the shore. They were quite still, waiting for Misha's command. Misha speculated that probably, all along this Pripet salient, partisan units like his were arriving. He wondered vaguely how this day, starting under its protective mist, would end. Would it matter to the colossal war effort, to history, to anyone, or would the partisan effort be like a bee stinging an elephant?

He grunted impatiently and gave the signal to start over the bridge, leading the way at a fast clip, zigzagging across and diving into the bushes on the far shore. Mottele and the others followed quickly, one by one, duplicating Misha's running style. The other side was strangely quiet. Misha moved his men inland about a hundred yards, had them sequester the few horses and dig trenches. Then, in the eerie mist, they waited in the trenches, their machine guns and rifles pointing in the direction of the coming action. They listened for the sounds of war.

In a trench with Mottele and Lyonka, Misha watched for the war through captured field glasses; now and then he passed them to the others, and Mottele peered through them briefly before handing them back. Outwardly the boy remained as composed as his comrades; but he was bursting inside with tension and anticipation, feeling that the world today was worth fighting for—weren't they about to grind the faces of tyrants and murderers? This was the day to settle accounts! And the boy felt the excitement of vengeance, like some heady *Kiddush* wine, course through his body.

Misha could hardly contain his impatience—for there was nothing to be seen. Nothing moved. Even the tall, staid trees, freshly leafed, were completely still, as though waiting mutely with them. The world around was alive with men on the mark, anxious for the war to explode and get on with it—but where was the war?

"When the action begins, Mottele," said Misha, "I want you to stay back and take care of the wounded, if there should be any."

"All right."

"You're to be on hand here, to take things back over the bridge—understand?"

"I understand, Uncle Misha. But you can't tell."

"What?"

"We might have to improvise—like at Ovruch with that German officers' club."

"We might."

The *chutzpah* of the boy! Misha had to chuckle to himself.

Then, without warning, the waiting was over.

An enemy plane flew past the partisans, circled the area and returned to the east. Two more planes followed, and now in the distance bombing could be heard. The planes were giving cover to their ground troops. Misha watched the action through his field glasses, and saw that the whole area was beginning to explode with war, and that his unit would be overwhelmingly outnumbered.

He couldn't tell how distant other partisan detachments might be—or whether the projected ambush was some Russian general's projected fantasy! He would have to get his men back a bit, nearer to the bridge, to give them a fighting chance, even prepare to blow up the bridge to stop the Germans from crossing. For a moment's fraction, Misha hesitated. He hated to draw his men back too soon, for there might be a way to make a stand. . . . Then a grenade came close, and that settled the matter.

He signaled to his men in the trenches, shouting, "Come on, tell the others! We're moving to the bushes, near the river! Get going!" Crouching as they ran, the partisans hid in the dense groves and waited again.

The bombings were becoming clearer, but still in the distance. Misha could see that the Germans were stopping and starting, flattening themselves on the ground to return the fire of the Russians. The enemy planes came over again, dangerously low now, skimming the treetops. But the planes weren't immune to the Russian counteroffensive: two of them caught fire and went screaming off to certain destruction. The third— had it exhausted its ammunition?—turned around and faded in the east.

Misha, watching the game of battlefield warfare, was relieved and aghast. "But good God, Lyonka, some of those Germans seem to be just boys!"

"Well, they've got guts, stopping to give some of it back!"

"Like their boss ordered."

"What we'd give to have their boss here!" Lyonka said.

"You mean what *I'd* give!" Mottele cried.

"You? Well, then, here he is!" Lyonka said impulsively. He took out his small comb, pointed the narrow tines down, stuck it between his nose and upper lip, pulled a lock of hair down to his brows, and shoved his left arm forward in a rigid Nazi salute. Mottele shrieked with laughter, remembering the Hitler portrait in the officers' club, but Misha regarded both of them with the wrath of Moses.

"Get down! Get your bloody arm down, stupid!" he shouted. "Do you want a bullet from *our* men?"

"Come on, Papa," Lyonka protested. "Where's your sense of humor?" But he dropped into a crouch, and his hands were trembling as he positioned his rifle.

"Kibitzing at a time like this!" replied Misha.

"Sorry, Papa."

"Anyway, it was the wrong arm," Misha added, and the two men broke into smiles.

Lyonka sent a rueful look to Mottele, who had already stopped smiling. The three now gazed toward the enemy, and in the bushes every partisan stared toward the two lines—enemy and friendly—which were coming closer. The Germans seemed to be worrying as much about possible ambush at their rear as about attackers in front of them, for now and then they sent grenades toward the bridge. They burst short of the partisans' hideout, and the men held their fire, waiting for Misha's command.

"Look, Misha!" Mottele cried suddenly. "Over there, on the right!"

He directed Misha's attention to a thick growth of bushes toward which three Russian officers were crawling. Some distance behind, several Germans snaked after them, apparently unseen by the Russians.

"They're going to attack our officers, Misha!"

Diadia Misha tried shouting a warning to the Russians.

Lyonka and Mottele took up the shout, but it was impossible—they couldn't make themselves heard. Misha watched the drama helplessly through the field glasses: the Russians would be massacred. Mottele, thinking the same thing, reacted impulsively. Time to improvise, he decided, as he said, "I'll go and warn them!"

He darted from the bushes without waiting for Misha's permission, which he guessed he wouldn't get. He was confident. After all, he told himself as he ran, he had a lot of experience, as when Diadia Misha himself was wounded, and almost overtaken by the German convoy.

Now as he ran, doubled over, with his automatic in his right hand, he knew how to put on speed while zigzagging through the bushes. The dense thicket covered this whole part of the forest, and he felt well protected. His mind was empty except for the immediate objective—to warn the Russian officers—and satisfy his burning need for vengeance.

The boy threw himself among the Russians before the startled officers knew what had hit them, or could use their guns. Mottele wasted no words, but, gasping for breath and control, he pointed to the thin line of Germans creeping toward them. The soldiers opened up on the human snake with everything they had—grenades, machine guns, rifle fire. The noise from the thicket was deafening, and could easily be heard down to the partisan line, Mottele noted with satisfaction. Diadia Misha would get the message!

The snake seemed to die in its tracks, and now the ambush was on in full force.

The Germans started to catch it from all sides. The war sounds became thunderous. Mottele stayed with the Russians until the enemy began to react with fewer and fewer replies to the bombardment. At last the Russians relaxed, and stared at the boy with amazement. They asked him questions in Russian, about himself, about the partisans. They hugged him, and stroked his head, and forced vodka on him, and asked him again and again about his comrades and the bridge.

Mottele was just as delighted with his new friends. He worried a bit about the scolding he was sure to get from Diadia Misha for rushing off, but his improvising had succeeded, hadn't it? and wasn't that what mattered? All he was guilty of was doing a *mitzva*— a good deed—right? he argued inwardly, as, feeling more and more subdued, he considered his punishment.

"All right, lad, one *mitzva* leads to another *mitzva*, as the saying goes," he could imagine Misha retorting. "You're going to be confined to the family camp." Surely not that!

Mottele stayed with the officers until the sounds of war from both sides died down, then he told them he had to get back to his unit. He would meet the Russians later, and he was eager to see their meeting with his commander, Captain Misha, he said.

He saluted the officers.

They stood at attention and saluted Mottele.

The boy went into his crouching run, and started through the bushes to Misha and Lyonka. He was almost all the way back when the German bullet tore into him. Misha and Lyonka saw him fall, and they ran to get him.

They brought Mottele to their hideout, and the men took off their jackets and laid the boy down on them and knelt beside him. The ground was muddy, and twigs snapped as they tried to make Mottele comfortable. The boy could see that the hideout was filled with tramped-over leaves and empty shells, and it smelled of smoke. The grenades must have come close.

Mottele looked into the strained faces of his two beloved comrades. He leaned toward Lyonka, who took the boy in his arms.

"I wanted to be with you," Mottele whispered.

"You're going to be all right," said Lyonka.

"I thought Misha will say I did a *mitzva.*"

"That's what I say, lad," Misha told him, as he fought back his emotion.

"Then I won't be banished to family camp?"

"No fear!"

Misha's hearty reaction raised a wan smile from the boy.

"We got to their boss, didn't we, Lyonka?"

"We did, Mottele, we sure did."

"I will tell them"—the boy's voice suddenly rose in a glad cry
—"I will tell my parents and my sister, Batya, that we took
revenge!"

Then Mottele sank back, and died in Lyonka's arms.

Lyonka held Mottele to him, until Misha finally took the boy
away, and put him down on the jackets again, and closed his
eyes.

All through the rest of the fighting, which lasted more
than an hour before the last shot was fired and the Germans done with, Misha and Lyonka fought with the rest of
the partisans. They waited until they saw the Russians come
running toward them to the safety of the bridge, and
other Russians driving forward in their vehicles. Then Misha
and Lyonka put down their guns and knelt again beside
Mottele.

"This was my brother, Papa," Lyonka said at last, "but I feel
nothing. Papa, what's wrong with me?"

"It's too soon to feel anything, Lyonka."

Misha stared from the dead boy to his son. Jacob yesterday,
Mottele's turn today. Tomorrow . . . ?

"Why can't I feel something?" Lyonka moaned.

"Don't, Lyonka."

"Why? Why?"

"I don't know. It's hard to feel anything in this place. There
are too many dead all around, and it's too soon. Mottele was a
brother, a son, a soldier, all at the same time, and more than
that, he was a Jew—one of ours. It's just too soon, Lyonka. We'll
have to give ourselves time."

Misha looked wearily out to the forest, and with his naked eye
now he could see what had been the battlefield. The ruins of
war were plain. The cost has been too heavy, he thought. The
cost is unbearable this day.

This day, which had begun under a heavy mist, now cleared.
The tall trees, towering over the scene and lacing the horizon,
threw no shadows. They were the only symbol of permanence
in this field of horror.

"At least it's over for Mottelê," said Misha.

"It will never be over for me," said Lyonka.

"For *us,*" said Misha. "Come, we must go. We have to tell the others."

EPILOGUE

At the end of the war, Captain Misha
né Moshe Gildenman of Korets in Volyn kept a
promise. He got to Berlin, and saw the remains
of the Hitler bunker which had been blown up.
Later, on a wall in Hitler's villa in Berchtesgaden,
he printed in large Hebrew letters:

"I, Moses, the son of Asher Halevi,
have outlived you, after you had condemned
me to death. The Jewish people live!"